HE LEADETH ME

HE LEADETH ME

Walter J. Ciszek, S.J.
with Daniel L. Flaherty, S.J.

IGNATIUS PRESS   SAN FRANCISCO

Originally published by Doubleday & Company, Inc.
Garden City, New York, 1973

Cover art by Christopher J. Pellicano
Cover design by Roxanne Mei Lum

Published by arrangement with Doubleday,
A division of Bantam Doubleday Dell Publishing Group, Inc.
Reprinted 1995, Ignatius Press, San Francisco
ISBN 978-0-89870-546-1
Library of Congress catalogue number 94-73067
Printed in the United States of America

The Lord's my shepherd, I'll not want
He makes me down to lie
In pastures green He leadeth me
The quiet waters by.
Yea, though I walk through death's valley
Yet will I fear no ill,
For Thou art with me and Thy rod
And staff me comfort still.

To my Russian friends,

Nikolai
Andrei
Ivan
Albert
Giorgi
Vladimir
Katia
Victor
Yekaterina

May He lead them as He led me.

And to my sister Helen Gearhart and my
dear friend Father Edward McCawley, S.J.,
whom He already leads.

CONTENTS

PROLOGUE

On October 12, 1963, I landed at New York's Idlewild Airport after having spent twenty-three years in the Soviet Union and most of that time in prison or the slave labor camps of Siberia. Some of my friends and family on hand that day said that I stepped off BOAC flight no. 501 like some new Columbus, about to rediscover America and take up again the life of a free man. I felt nothing of that. Nor did I know that I had officially been listed as dead since 1947 and that my Jesuit colleagues had said Masses for the repose of my soul when it was thought I had died in a Soviet prison. I felt only a simple sense of gratitude to God for having sustained me through those years and, in his providence, bringing me home again at last.

It was shortly after I left home and family in Shenandoah, Pennsylvania, to join the Jesuits in 1928 that I first volunteered for the "Russian missions". Pope Pius XI wrote a letter in 1929 to all seminarians, "especially our Jesuit sons", asking for men to enter a new Russian center being started at Rome to prepare young clerics for possible future work in Russia. I studied my theology there and learned to say Mass in the Byzantine rite in preparation for work in Russia. But after I was ordained, there was no way to send priests into Russia, so I was assigned instead to an Oriental rite mission staffed by Jesuits in Albertyn, Poland.

I was working there when war broke out in September 1939. The German Army took Warsaw, but the Red Army overran eastern Poland and Albertyn. In the confusion and aftermath of these invasions, I followed many Polish refugees into Russia. Disguised as a worker, I accompanied them in the hope of being able to minister to their spiritual needs. But I didn't fool the Soviet secret police. As soon as Germany invaded Russia in June 1941, I was picked up by the NKVD and put into prison.

I was taken by train to the dread Lubianka Prison in Moscow for interrogation as a "Vatican spy". I remained there all through the war years, undergoing periodic and often intense questioning by the NKVD. Then, after five years, I was sentenced to fifteen years at hard labor in the prison camps of Siberia. Along with thousands of others, I was put to work in labor brigades doing outdoor construction in the extreme arctic cold, or in coal and copper mines, ill clothed, ill fed, and poorly housed in the timber barracks surrounded by barbed wire and a "death zone". Men died in those camps, especially those who gave up hope. But I trusted in God, never felt abandoned or without hope, and survived along with many others. I never looked on my survival as anything special or extraordinary, but I did give thanks to God for sustaining and preserving me through those years.

When my term at last ran out, I was not completely free. Because I had been "convicted" on a charge of espionage, I could not leave Siberia and return to the main cities of Russia, let alone leave the country. So I remained in the villages and towns of Siberia, working as an auto mechanic among other things, until I was finally exchanged in 1963 for two convicted Russian spies, thanks to the efforts of family and friends and the good offices of the US State Department. Upon my arrival, my religious superiors and a number of publishers convinced me that there was a great deal of public interest in the story of my years inside the Soviet Union, those years when I had actually been given up for dead. So I agreed to tell that story and did so in the book *With God in Russia.*

Yet, to be perfectly honest, that was not the book I wanted to write. I felt that I had learned much during those years of hardship and suffering that could be of help to others in their lives. For every man's life contains its share of suffering; each of us is occasionally driven almost to despair, to ask why God allows evil and suffering to overtake him or those he loves. I had seen a great deal of suffering in the camps and the prisons in those around me, had almost despaired myself, and had learned in those darkest of hours to turn to God for consolation and to trust in him alone.

"How did you manage to survive?" is the question most often asked me by newsmen and others ever since my return home. My answer has always been the same: "God's providence". Yet I knew that simple statement could never satisfy the questioner or ever begin to convey all I meant by it. Through the long years of isolation and suffering, God had led me to an understanding of life and his love that only those who have experienced it can fathom. He had stripped away from me many of the external consolations, physical and religious, that men rely on and had left me with a core of seemingly simple truths to guide me. And yet what a profound difference they had made in my life, what strength they gave me, what courage to go on! I wanted to tell others about them—indeed, I felt one reason that God in his providence had brought me safely home was so that I might help others understand these truths a little better.

So, even in the pages of that first book, *With God in Russia,* I tried to say something of what I had learned and felt I must say, to give some hint at least of the truths that had guided and sustained me. I knew I had not done it adequately or properly within the limitations of those pages, but I was consoled by the many letters and personal requests for spiritual guidance I received, which indicated that somehow readers of that story had read far more between the lines than I had been able to say. I knew then that I must someday write this book.

I also knew, though, that I could not do it alone. Strong as the motivations were that compelled me to write it, strong as were my desires, I knew only too well that my limited talents as a writer were inadequate to the task. I never considered myself a writer, and I never will. Yet the idea of the message I had to communicate and share with others was so strong within me that, after two years of hesitation, I turned once more to Father Daniel L. Flaherty, S.J., who had been such a help to me in producing the first book, and explained to him my ideas and my dreams for this book. To me he is more than a collaborator or excellent editor; in the few brief years I have known him and worked with him, he has become one of my closest friends, almost a part of my soul. If he had said no, I think I would have abandoned there and then any idea of further writing once and for all. But he didn't say no. He agreed to help me again, and his encouragement fostered my enthusiasm to push ahead.

I found, however, that this was a far more difficult book to write—and it took me a long time to put into words what I felt I wanted to say. It took even longer sometimes for Dan to understand me, for it is hard for one man to catch another's spirit and put into print the things that drive him on. Yet somehow, with God's help, the prayers of many friends, and Dan's patient collaboration, this book has at last taken shape and is ready to appear in print, God willing, after months of persistent effort. And now that it has finally been completed, I can only hope and pray it proves helpful to those who may read it.

If so, I want to take occasion here to express my thanks and deep gratitude to all who helped me in so many ways—with their prayers and with their material and moral support—to finish a task I feared all along to tackle alone. I think it is obvious how deeply indebted I am to Dan for giving me so much of his time and energy to accomplish what I felt had to be done. I am also indebted to Father John B. Amberg, S.J., for permitting me to live at Canisius House, the Jesuit house of writers in Evanston connected with Loyola University Press, and for letting me spend over half a year there seriously engaged in the final preparation of this manuscript. I am no less indebted to all the members of the Canisius House community for tolerating my presence and helping by their congeniality to make my stay with them a most pleasant and productive experience, a time I shall never forget. I owe my deepest thanks of all, of course, to the members of the community of the John XXIII Center for Eastern studies at Fordham University, of which I am a member. It was they who agreed to let me be absent from the community for over six months and spend the time in writing, while they took upon themselves the responsibilities of fulfilling the work I would have had to perform as an active member of the community if present. Sincere thanks, too, to Mary Helen O'Neill for the generous

contributions she made to aid me throughout the long and difficult process of writing. Last of all, my deep gratitude to all those
not mentioned by name for all the help, large and small, they
offered me during this time. To all, my prayers and good wishes.

WALTER J. CISZEK, S.J.
Canisius House
July 31, 1972
Feast of St. Ignatius Loyola

Chapter One

ALBERTYN

"The Red Army is here. They've taken the town. The Soviets are here." The news spread like panic through the small village of Albertyn, Poland, on October 17, 1939. I had just finished Mass and breakfast on that memorable morning when bewildered parishioners came to the mission to tell me the news. It was news we had feared ever since it had become clear that Germany and Russia were dividing up Poland. But now our fears were a reality. The Red Army was in Albertyn.

One by one the parishioners came crowding to the mission to ask my opinion, to seek my advice, looking for a word of hope or consolation. They were worried about their families. They were worried about their sons in the Polish Army, or their husbands in the government. They were worried about their children and what would happen to them all. I tried to be reassuring, but what could I really say? I had no answers to their immediate questions of fact, and how could I reassure them about the future or comfort them in the midst of the turmoil that had overtaken the town? What could I tell them except to pray and to trust in God?

Even in that I felt foolish. I had been with them a little more than a year, I had been ordained a little more than two years, How inexperienced and immature I felt at this sudden crisis of such proportions. Supported by the routines of a parish priest, I had ministered to these people in their daily problems, helped them, consoled them, said Mass and brought Communion to the sick, anointed the dying. I had made many friends among them, and they trusted me, young as I was—the young American in their midst. But the war changed everything. The crises they faced now were not family quarrels or sickness or the loss of a loved one. The advice they wanted now was not about things common to every parish and learned by every priest. Suddenly, our whole world, theirs and mine, had changed.

It is impossible to describe the feeling that comes over you at such a time. The feeling that somehow, in an instant of time, everything is changed and nothing again will ever be quite the same. That tomorrow will never again be like yesterday. That the very trees, the grass, the air, the daylight are no longer the same, for the world has changed. It is a feeling impossible to describe, and yet one that every wife who has lost a husband knows well, one that every child who has tasted evil for the first time or faced a sudden crisis has experienced. It is that feeling that leaves the heart saying, "Oh, if only I could turn back the clock to before it happened, if only it had never happened, if only I had it to do over again."

My fears were vague that morning, though the feeling of inadequacy was very real. And the fears themselves quickly ceased to be vague and became quite real in turn. Arrests soon followed the arrival of the Red Army. Property was confiscated. There were countless interrogations, threats, and intimidations, as the communists endeavored to round up everyone they considered a threat to them or to their new order.

In all this, the Church itself became a special target for attack. The Oriental rite church at our mission was closed immediately; the Latin rite parish was allowed to function for a while for those few families who dared to attend. The rest of our mission buildings were taken over by the Red Army and used to quarter troops. A propaganda campaign was mounted against the Church and against the priests; we labored under a campaign of constant harassment and incidents large and small. And it was effective. Even the most faithful became cautious about visiting the church or seeing a priest. Young people dropped away quickly. Workers soon learned they could lose their jobs if they insisted upon attending religious services. Our activity as priests was limited strictly to the church; we could not go to the people unless they came to us. Few of them dared to do so. Soon our ministry consisted solely of saying Mass on Sunday for a few old people. The Jesuit mission, which had flourished for ten years in Albertyn, was destroyed in a matter of weeks.

Again and again, as I watched all this happen, I had to force myself not to think of the question that kept returning unbidden to mind: "Why has God allowed this evil to happen?" Why persecutions? If God must allow natural disasters, or even wars because of human failings, why can't he at least allow his flock to be shepherded and comforted during such calamities? Surely he could defend and protect his flock instead of having it singled out for special attack such as this. The perplexity and pain grew within me as I saw the visible Church, once strong and organized, dissolve under the attacks of these invaders and watched the people grow estranged, pressured ceaselessly into accepting this new order. And what of the young people who were literally torn away from their parents and forced to join the Young Pioneers or Komsomol organizations, taught to report on any "deviations" of the old people at home? How frustrating it was to hear the Church and priests and religious openly slandered in communist propaganda, and to know that the children had to learn and repeat atheist doctrines every day in school and in their class work. How could God allow all this? And why?

I did not blame the people. I knew they had not lost their faith but were just afraid right now to practice it openly. They came to me at night to ask how they should conduct themselves, to ask whether it was wrong to cooperate with the new order, to ask if they should let their children join the Komsomol organizations, or whether they themselves should join the labor unions. And finally, they came to ask whether, under the circumstances, it was wrong not to come to church on Sundays or feast days. And what could I tell them? How much heroism could I ask of them? How much did God, who had allowed all this to happen, expect of these simple, ordinary people of the backwoods of Albertyn?

It was agony for me as a priest to ask these questions, but it was impossible not to ask them. They crowded to mind in times of prayer, they came at Mass, they came all through the days and nights. And I'm sure they came not to me alone. It was not a crisis of faith, any more than it is for anyone who has ever suffered a great loss or faced a family tragedy and asked himself the same questions. It was rather a crisis of understanding, and no one need be ashamed to admit he has been troubled by it. Anyone who has done much reading in the Old Testament is familiar with those questions. "How long, O Lord, how long will you allow our enemies to triumph over us?" Most especially in the days after David, in the ages of captivity, when the glories of the golden age of Solomon were but a memory by the rivers of Babylon and Israel had been broken and led away in shame, does the question recur again and again. To Israel, surely, it must have seemed the end of the world, the end of the covenant, the end of God's special care for his chosen people.

Yet, from our vantage point in history, we know it was really quite the opposite. Israel's troubles were in truth a manifestation of Yahweh's special providence, his special love for his chosen people. Like a fond and loving father, he was trying to wean them away from trust in kings or princes or in armies or the powers of this world. He was trying to teach them, again and again, that their faith must only be in him alone. He was leading them, through every trial and in every age, to the realization that God alone is faithful in all tribulations, that he alone is constant in his love and must be clung to, even when it seems all else has been turned upside down. Yahweh is still the Lord behind the events and happenings of this world; he can be found there and he must be sought in them, so that his will may be done. It was he who had chosen them, not they him. It was he who had first made the covenant with them, who had led them and cared for them, shepherded and fed and guarded them in every tribulation. Their part in the covenant must be to trust in him alone, to remain always faithful, to look to him and not to other gods, to rely on him and not on rulers or on chariots or bowmen. He was ever faithful and so in turn must they be, even when he led them where they would not go, into a land they knew not, or into exile. For he had chosen them, they were his people, he would no more forget them than a mother could forget the child of her womb— yet neither, in their turn, must they ever forget him.

This is a hard lesson. And the Old Testament is a chronicle of the many times and the many ways God tried to teach that lesson to his chosen people. And it is a record, too, of how very often, in times of peace and prosperity, Israel came to take Yahweh for granted, to settle down in some routine and to accept the status quo as the be-all and the end-all, to think of the established order as their support and sustenance, and to forget their ultimate goal and destiny as the people of the covenant. Then Yahweh would have to remind them again, by the downfall of the monarchy or by exile or the destruction of Jerusalem, that he alone must be their ultimate hope, their sole source of support, for he had chosen them out of all the people of the world to be a sign of his power and his love, and they must testify to him before all the world by the witness of their trust in him alone.

That same lesson each of us must learn, difficult or not. How easy it is, in times of ease, for us to become dependent on our routines, on the established order of our day-to-day existence, to carry us along. We begin to take things for granted, to rely on ourselves and on our own resources, to "settle in" in this world and look to it for our support. We all too easily come to equate being comfortable with a sense of well-being, to seek our comfort solely in the sense of being comfortable. Friends and possessions surround us, one day is followed by the next, good health and happiness for the most part are ours. We don't have to desire much of the things of this world—to be enamored of riches, for example, or greedy or avaricious—in order to have gained this sense of comfort and of well-being, to trust in them as our support—and to take God for granted. It is the status quo that we rely on, that carries us from day to day, and somehow we begin to lose sight of the fact that under all these things and behind all those things it is God who supports and sustains us. We go along, taking for granted that tomorrow will be very much like today, comfortable in the world we have created for ourselves, secure in the established order we have learned to live with, however imperfect it may be, and give little thought to God at all.

Somehow, then, God must contrive to break through those routines of ours and remind us once again, like Israel, that we are ultimately dependent only upon him, that he has made us and destined us for life with him through all eternity, that the things of this world and this world itself are not our lasting city, that his we are and that we must look to him and turn to him in everything. Then it is, perhaps, that he must allow our whole world to be turned upside down in order to remind us it is not our permanent abode or final destiny, to bring us to our senses and restore our sense of values, to turn our thoughts once more to him—even if at first our thoughts are questioning and full of reproaches. Then it is that he must remind us again, with terrible clarity, that he meant exactly what he said in those seemingly simple words of the Sermon on the Mount: "Do not be anxious about what you shall eat, or what you shall wear, or where you shall sleep, but seek first the kingdom of God and his justice."

So it was with the people of Israel, who must learn not to put their trust in princes or in kingdoms but to be faithful only to Yahweh as he was ever faithful to them, and to put all their trust in him. So it has been throughout the history of the New Testament. There have been changes and upheavals in the Church herself, there have been persecutions. It is not princes or rulers, structures or organizations, that sustain the Church. It is God who sustains her. So must it be in Albertyn. God is constant in his love if we will but look to him, he will sustain us in every storm if we will but cry out to him, he will save us if we will but reach out our hand to him. He is there, if we will only turn to him and learn to trust in him alone. The upheavals in this world, or in the Church herself, are not the end of everything, especially of his love. They can in fact serve best as signs to remind us of his love and of his constancy, to make us turn once more to him and cling to him again when all else that we counted on is overturned around us.

And so it is in each of our lives. It is a sad commentary on our human frailty that we fail to think of God or see him behind the comfortable routines of our day-to-day existence. It is only in a crisis that we remember him and turn to him, often as querulous and questioning children. It is in moments of loss or family tragedy or personal despair that men turn to him and ask, "Why?" —indeed are almost forced to turn to him, again and at last, for help and for support and consolation. Mysteriously, God in his providence must make use of our tragedies to remind our fallen human nature of his presence and his love, of the constancy of his concern and care for us. It is not vindictiveness on his part; he does not send us tragedies to punish us for having so long forgotten him. The failing is on our part. He is always present and ever faithful; it is we who fail to see him or to look for him in times of ease and comfort, to remember he is there, shepherding and guarding and providing us the very things we come to count on and expect to sustain us every day. Yet we fail to remember that, comfortable as we are in our established order and the status quo, as day follows day.

So it was in Albertyn, as the war tore apart the fabric of our once peaceful lives, my own included, that I came to understand more clearly and in some small way this truth in all its terrible simplicity: "Do not be anxious, therefore, saying what shall we eat or what shall we wear, or where shall we sleep, for your heavenly Father knows that you need all these things. Seek first the kingdom of God and his justice." We would survive, although the world around us had changed completely. We would go on, today and tomorrow and the next day, picking up the pieces and working out each day our eternal destiny and our salvation. There would be a tomorrow, and we would have to live in it—and God would be there as well. The Church would survive, perhaps not exactly as we had known it at the mission, because the faith would survive among the people of God as it had always survived in times of persecution. One thing only need be of great concern to us in all this seeming upheaval and catastrophe: to be faithful to God and to look to him in everything, confident of his love and his constancy, aware that this world and this new order was not our lasting city any more than the previous one had been, and striving always to know his will and to do it each day of our lives.

Chapter Two

THE DECISION TO ENTER RUSSIA

In the midst of the wartime upheaval that was Albertyn, Father Makar suddenly appeared one evening like a bolt from the blue. Makar, a mischievous Georgian with long wavy hair, hooked nose, and flashing black eyes, had been a student with me at the Russian College in Rome before the war and a constant companion. Now he had been sent by our Jesuit superior to Lvov to tell us that the bishop had decided, under the circumstances, to close the Oriental rite mission in Albertyn for the time being. Our reunion in this war-torn town was an emotional one. Father Makar threw his arms about me and embraced me with all his might; he gave me the triple kiss, European style. My reaction was equally warm and exuberant.

Makar had come, however, with more in mind than the message about the closing of the mission. He had asked to be the one to deliver that message because he wanted to sound me out on the possibility of going into Russia. He told me that he and Father Victor Nestrov, another of my classmates from our years at the Russicum, had discussed with their superiors the possibility of Jesuits accompanying labor brigades to the Soviet Union in order to minister to their needs. The plan was simple enough. The Soviets were hiring large numbers from the occupied zones to work in Russian factories around the Ural Mountains. They had also been rounding up suspects of all kinds and shipping them off to work camps in the Urals. Makar and Nestrov talked quite simply of going with some of these laborers across the Russian border. But they knew I would want to join them. The three of us had been nicknamed "the three musketeers" by our other classmates in Rome. Even then, they had kidded us about our incessantly expressed desire to go to Russia—and that was the proposal Father Makar brought me along with the news that the bishop was closing the Oriental rite mission in Albertyn.

The moment Makar spoke of going to Russia my heart leapt. I was so excited, so seized by a deep interior joy, that I had to restrain my emotions in order not to seem foolish. If I let myself go, I thought, I will act silly. I was so elated I could hardly speak. And yet, in that very moment of elation and joy, I knew what my answer would be. I had no doubts, no fears, no hesitation. I knew what I was going to do next, what I had wanted all my life, what the mission to Albertyn had been meant for in God's providence.

And not just the mission at Albertyn. It was as if my whole life, in God's plan, had pointed to this moment. I could remember vividly that day so long ago, during the second year of my noviceship at St. Andrew's in New York, when our novice master read us a letter from Pius XI asking for volunteers to join a new Russian mission just opened in Rome. Even as he read the letter, something within me stirred. I could hardly wait for the conference to finish so I could go to the novice master and volunteer for this new Russian apostolate. I remember telling him, "Father, when you read the Pope's letter in there just now it was almost like a direct call from God. I knew I had to volunteer for this Russian mission. I knew it from the very beginning, and as you kept on reading, that feeling grew until at the end I was fully convinced that God was calling me, that Russia was my destination in God's providence. I knew—I firmly believe!—that God wants me there and I will be there in the future."

Of course the novice master had been skeptical of such enthusiasm from a young novice. And yet that vision of the call to Russia never left me. I never considered it an illusion, and it influenced every moment of my life. It was something intangible, sometimes consciously remembered and at other times unconsciously acted upon, but it was very real. It was to me what God's call to the patriarch Abraham must have been, that call by which he was told to leave his kinfolk in Ur of the Chaldees and journey to a land the Lord would show him. It made it possible for me to leave my family and friends, to leave my Jesuit classmates in the United States, and go to Rome to study at the Russicum. I was lonely enough and homesick in the years that followed. My father died while I was studying in Rome, and I could not be at his funeral. When I was at last ordained in Rome, none of my family could afford to make the trip to be with me. Yet through those years I never once wavered in my conviction that God had called me for the Russian missions; I never doubted that I would one day serve him there.

So one of my greatest disappointments came shortly after ordination, when I was told it was impossible for the moment to send men into Russia. I was assigned instead to the Oriental rite mission at Albertyn. It was an emotional letdown—after all I had sacrificed, studied for, dreamed about, and trained for—yet even then, in that moment of extreme disappointment, I never doubted it was God's will that I would one day be in Russia. And here was Makar, asking me if I was ready to accompany him and Father Nestrov across the Russian border! When I was calm enough to trust myself to speak, I almost shouted: "Of course, of course! We'll go together. We'll be in Russia in the spring!"

I was elated and Makar, the happy-go-lucky Georgian, was the perfect companion for my mood. We talked and talked; the plans he described were my plans. It was strange, we said, how God's providence worked in mysterious ways. The Russian armies had overrun Poland and the mission at Albertyn, so I was already to some extent inside Russia. The Russians had come to me, so what was to prevent me from going to them in return, even though it meant crossing a border forbidden to priests? And did not the bishop's closing of the Oriental rite mission at Albertyn free me from any responsibility to remain here longer? The refugees needed priests in Russia, crossing the border with them looked easy enough, our mission here was hampered by Red troops—it was all so providential that the will of God seemed clear.

Despite my excitement, I sensed this was a moment of the greatest importance. It was a turning point, a new departure, and it was going to influence my whole future life. Yet it was what I had always wanted, hoped for, dreamed about since that day at St.

Andrew's. I was more than ever certain now it was the will of God for me. And underneath all my happy discussion with Makar of future plans, I felt again that immense joy, that deep interior peace, that intense conviction I had felt when first I heard the call to the Russian apostolate on that day years ago.

It was not to be that easy, though. The next morning brought with it a flood of second thoughts. Had I let my enthusiasm for an old dream run away with my better judgment? Could I be so sure of God's will? Wasn't I interpreting the present situation as a "sign" of God's providence only because I wanted it to be that way? Wasn't I merely following my own desires and simply calling them God's will for me? Anyone who has ever wrestled with his conscience over a particular course of action has experienced what I went through then. Any young man or woman who has felt called to a vocation and then hesitated, wondering if the call is genuine, knows the agonies of such second thoughts and how powerful the counter arguments can be.

Reasons and rationalizations boil through your mind. There are present and future responsibilities toward family and friends to think of, thoughts of the good to be done at home or in other possible ways of serving God and man, mistrust about the motives swaying the mind now this way and now that, doubts about one's abilities to live up to the call (and even about the call itself), vague fears for the future and very real fears of making a mistake right here and now, knowing a decision must be made and yet knowing, too, that it involves a commitment from which there can be no turning back, something that will change the whole course of your life. Men faced with the possibility of a new and perhaps better job, women considering a proposal to marry, parents planning a move of one sort or another, teenagers trying to decide their future in a changing world—all knowing the troubling turmoil of doubts and fears, of competing reasons and of answers, that can afflict the mind and paralyze the will in such a situation.

So it was with me then. And the most chilling argument was this: Was I not running away from my responsibility to the parishioners at Albertyn? Was I the hireling who flees and leaves the sheep untended in time of danger? True, the Oriental rite mission was being closed by the bishop. But the Latin rite parish remained. The people, especially the old people, still braved persecution to come to Mass. Could I be any less courageous? Is it not the first obligation of a priest to remain with his flock in all situations, but especially when danger threatens them? Was I so sure God wanted me to go into Russia? Hadn't he arranged it, so to speak, that I was already in Russia? Could I really believe that God wanted me to leave this very real situation, these very real needs of his people in Albertyn, to go chasing some will-of-the-wisp in an unknown land among people who had not sought for help or asked me to come? How could I be so certain of God's will?

I was tortured by these questions and these arguments. They made sense both logically and spiritually, and I knew they were more than mere rationalizations. The mind comes up with rationalizations to justify for itself a decision taken without sufficient reason, or to justify doing what the will has already determined for itself that it is going to do. That is why such rationalizations are so often suspect, why motives must always be examined so carefully. But these were arguments *against* doing what I knew I wanted to do, these were questions based on fact and on reality, and they were valid arguments. Everyone who has had to weigh the choice of a vocation against the call of family, or who has had to weigh the value of some future course or vision against the demanding realities of the present, knows the force of the dilemma that troubled me then. Abraham, called by God to leave behind everything he knew and cherished in order to set out for an unknown land on the strength of a vague promise, must have known the full force of such counter arguments. Or again, when called by God to sacrifice his son Isaac, who embodied the very fulfillment of that original promise, how could Abraham be so sure of the will of God? How can anyone be sure?

I remember that crisis well. I had never before doubted that it was God's will for me to go to Russia. From the day I first heard the call, that conviction had formed the core of my life. This belief, this absolute faith in God's providence, had sustained me in all difficulties, had carried me through all disappointments. I had dreamed of it, hoped for it, trusted in it, given myself up to it, found comfort in it—and now I was faced with this spiritual dilemma. Was I really so certain of God's will? Or was I really so sure, at least, that this opportunity to go into Russia was God's will for me right now?

I turned to prayer, but my mind was in such turmoil, my intellect so actively involved in weighing reasons pro and con, that I could not hear the voice of God. I talked it over with Makar and also with Father Grybowski, the only priest from the mission who would be left in Albertyn if I were to leave. I talked to the parishioners, who begged me not to go. Finally, I decided I could not leave Albertyn. I could not leave a church where I knew I was wanted. I could not leave a parish whose needs I knew intimately, I could not run from danger or from persecution, in order to follow a vague and largely idealistic vision of future service in a distant land to an unknown flock. God, through my superiors, had assigned me to Albertyn; that much of his will was certain. In Albertyn, therefore, I would stay.

Yet hardly had I made that decision, in all sincerity and with firm conviction, than I was again distraught. I felt no peace, no joy, no ease of heart at having finally resolved my problem. Prayer became difficult, almost impossible. I felt my faith was weakened, that I had come to this decision by listening to the voice of reason rather than by listening to the voice of God. I was distracted by the feeling I had broken a pattern that had dominated my whole life up till now. For this decision was a break with the way I had always experienced and interpreted the workings of divine providence in my life, had always striven to see God's will in everything and to follow it. Most important, however, was the loss of that deep interior sense of peace, that sense of joy and enthusiasm, that strong spirit of faith in God's involvement in my life which, up to now, had been such an integral part of all my spirituality.

Accordingly, I was led once more to reconsider the decision to remain at Albertyn. I prayed that I might be totally open to God's providence, that I would trust only in him, that like Abraham I would be prepared to follow his call no matter where it might lead, without thoughts of self or doubts or reasons of my own. I wanted to be totally open to God's will, to hear his voice, and to leave self out of it. That was my prayer for guidance. And immediately there came flooding back that sense of peace, that feeling of joy, that confidence in the simple and direct faith expressed in trusting him alone. I knew then what I must do. I experienced then what I had heard before from spiritual directors or read in spiritual books but never fully understood: that God's will can be discerned by the fruits of the spirit it brings, that peace of soul and joy of heart are two such signs, provided they follow upon total commitment and openness to God alone and are not founded on the self's desires. That the validity of a call can be tested—whether it be the call of a vocation or of some new departure within that vocation—by the movements of soul that accompany it. That the movements of God's grace must always be accepted and understood in virtue of the life of faith, because ultimately the truth of every mysterious action of his grace is discerned in the light of faith rather than by the powers of reason or of intellect.

There are movements of the soul, deeper than words can describe and yet more powerful than any reason, which can give a man to know beyond question or arguing or doubt that "*digitus Dei est hic* [the finger of God is here]", and the name of that reality is grace. God *does* inspire men by his grace, does lift the heart, does enlighten the mind and move the will. Faith is required to accept that reality, but it is a reality nonetheless. Not all the logic and reasoned explanations of the theologians may serve to convince those who do not have the gift of faith of that reality, but it remains a reality. For what it's worth, I can testify to that. Only in the decision to go on to Russia did I find the joy and the interior peace that are marks of God's true intervention in the soul. And so to Russia I would go.

Chapter Three

RUSSIA

"Look, Nestrov," I said, "look at the rich black soil we're passing now. There is no end to it." Then suddenly I cried, "Look at the signpost we just passed! It's the border of Russia." I leaped up off the wooden planks of the boxcars and cried to everyone inside, "We're in Russia!" Immediately everyone in the freight car was up, crowding at the entrance, peering out through the slats in the side of the car, looking back at the signpost that was already getting smaller and smaller as the train plowed slowly ahead. Despite the cramped wooden quarters of the car, everyone's spirits soared. Their faces lit up. They slapped one another on the back. Someone started to sing. But I fell silent, looking out at the rich soil of Russia for the first time, extremely moved. After a while, I turned to Father Nestrov and said quietly, "What did I tell you? Russia in the spring!" And then I added, almost as an afterthought, "Today is the nineteenth of March, the feast of St. Joseph the Worker."

Nestrov and I looked at each other for a long moment in silence. There was no way of knowing what the future would bring, but we were at last doing what we had dreamt so many years of doing, what we had discussed so often during our student days in Rome, what we had planned so carefully during the past months in Lvov. It didn't matter if no one else in that boxcar knew we were priests. We knew it. To them I was Wladimir Lypinski, a Pole whose family had been wiped out in a German air raid. Crossing the Russian border gave me a strange sense of exhilaration and yet of loneliness, of a beginning and an end. Even the land itself seemed different. The vast sweep of the Ukraine, with seemingly unlimited stretches of cultivated land rising at times to gently rolling hills and pastureland.

The enthusiasm of the others in the car was infectious, a combination of many causes. For one thing, it meant we were nearing the end of our trip in the roughhewn confines of boxcar 89725. There had been twenty-five of us in the car when the trip started, but other workers had been piled in at stops along the way. The car had two rows of rough plank bunks along the wall, straw on the floor, and a ventilator at the top of the car. The only other furnishings were an old punctured oil drum that served as a stove, and a slop bucket to serve as a toilet. We had been hired by Lespromhoz, a big Soviet lumber combine that was hiring men for work in the Ural regions. They were anxious to get cheap labor, especially refugees, from lands newly occupied by the Russian Army. Few questions were asked. The great majority of the people in our car were Jews who had fled before the Nazi advance into Poland. Whole families were on the train—grandfather, grandmother, father, mother, and children. Uprooted after generations, they were carrying everything they owned on their backs, like refugees everywhere, to a new life in an alien land. They talked for hours during the jolting stop-and-go trip that took better than two weeks, of the homes they had left and their new hopes. Together we talked about the opportunities that lay ahead of us in the Urals.

For all of us, therefore, crossing the border into Russia had a special meaning. For Father Nestrov and me it was the fulfillment of a dream. For Franck, a Warsaw Jew with whom Nestrov and I had become quite friendly on the trip, it was also the fulfillment of a dream. He was a communist who had fled from Warsaw just before it fell to the Germans. He had determined then to take his family—his wife, his ten-year-old son, and his nephew—to live in that paradise he had read so much about in communist literature. Each of the others in the car undoubtedly had reasons of his own for the joy that swept over us all in crossing the border into Russia. For my part, I will never forget that feeling. It was a mixture of natural elation at having reached a goal, coupled with a deep interior peace and joy. Enthusiasm and hope mingled with the sudden realization that I would now be cut off completely from the supports I had known—from my Jesuit superiors and colleagues, from my family, from the visible Church, from the power of the US Government to protect me in case of serious trouble. For a moment I thought with sorrow and regret about the possibility of never returning to Europe, to the United States, to Shenandoah. Yet the strong realization rushed over me that I was not cut off from God, that he was with me, indeed that I was dependent only on him in a new and very real way. My spirits soared, my heart beat a little faster with happiness at this realization, as I joined in the general celebration in that boxcar for special reasons of my own.

Our arrival in the Ural lumber towns of Chusovoy and Teplaya-Gora soon ended our euphoria. It was raining when we arrived, bone-weary and long since out of the food and provisions we had taken for the trip. Starving, we had to stand in the rain while a Lespromhoz representative checked us out and then slog through the mud to a camp a mile outside the city. At the camp, the barracks were new and raw. Large sections in the walls, where the timbers had warped, were stuffed with mud and a plaster-like stucco. The work we were assigned was rough. In mixed brigades of men and women, we hauled logs from the river and stacked them in rows over six feet high and some thirty yards in length. The pay was bad to start with, and it depended upon how many cubic meters of logs you stacked in a day. Newcomers, obviously, were not very good at the work and so earned very little. Nestrov and I, for example, pooled our salaries for food but sometimes had only enough to buy a loaf of rye bread. There were nights we couldn't even afford that, since we also had to pay for our lodging in the barracks and that was deducted before we even saw our paycheck. Our friend Franck, with his dreams of a worker's paradise, was stunned by it all.

Father Nestrov and I were equally disappointed. Not by the physical labor, exhausting as it was, or the constant discomfort, the wretched housing, the lack of privacy, or gnawing hunger. All these were difficult enough to bear, but we would have endured them gladly if we could have achieved our purpose for coming to Russia. The rudest awakening of all, however, was our growing realization that we might have no apostolate at all here. Though freedom of religion is technically guaranteed by the Soviet Constitution, proselytization is strictly forbidden. The constitution guarantees freedom of atheist propaganda, but those who try to spread the truths of the faith or foster religion are in fact breaking the law. Nestrov and I had known this, of course, simply as a matter of pure fact; now we began to experience it as a fact of daily life.

Nobody wanted to talk about religion, let alone practice it. Though none of the workers in our barracks knew that Nestrov and I were priests, they were still reluctant to so much as discuss any matters dealing with God or religion. We were accepted among them as fellow workers, in an easy spirit of comradeship. We shared the work, the poor food, the poor housing, the daily hardships. The refugees, especially, were a simple people with a difficult lot in life that they accepted with resignation. They welcomed us in their company, conversed freely, and answered practical problems with the clichés and bromides born of common hardships or cultural heritage. But they would not speak of God or hear of God.

They were afraid. Nestrov and I, too, became cautious and even fearful; you could not help it in that atmosphere. We were afraid not only for ourselves and for what we still hoped might prove the ultimate success of our apostolate, but for the people among whom we hoped to minister as well. They had so little in this life that we did not want to be the cause of further trouble to them. We knew, and they knew, there were informers and party members who would report any religious activities. It was even necessary not to say anything to the children about God, tempting as such a thought might be, lest they in all innocence tell others about our conversation and so give us away.

We had hoped, when we made our plans to come to Russia, that we could begin our apostolate by ministering to the refugees, many of whom would be Polish Catholics, and then gradually widen our influence to serve the believers still in Russia. Instead, we found we could not even bring up the subject of religion with our fellow workers, whether refugees or native Russians, let alone tell them we were priests. And as this realization dawned, our disappointment grew. Because our hopes had been so high, our enthusiasm so great, our disappointment at being unable to initiate any type of apostolate at all was just that much the greater. Disappointment gradually gave way to a feeling of disillusionment and depression. There were even times when I took pity on myself and thought harshly about my fellow workers. I had given up so much, sacrificed so much, risked so much in order to bring Christ to them—and would they not even talk to me about such things? "We will never get anywhere here", I sometimes said to Father Nestrov, "because the people are so full of fear." They would even hesitate to take the risk of having the children baptized in secret or of receiving the sacraments secretly. Yet these were the people I had come to serve, the people who were deprived of all means of worshiping God. I wanted to suffer with them and for them; if only they were willing to accept me, not as a fellow worker but as a priest!

At other times I felt humiliated. The zeal of the communists, I thought, put me to shame. And that they were effective there could be no doubt. Indeed, it was their very effectiveness that made me feel, as a priest, alien among my own people. I had come to serve and I could not serve, because no one would listen to me. What could Nestrov and I do against the power of this system? The notion that we could ever effectively work in this country, under these conditions, seemed in retrospect nothing but a pipe dream. We had entered upon what we thought was a great missionary endeavor, full of zeal and enthusiasm, only to come smack up against reality. Things here were not at all as we had envisioned them, and we were not at all equipped to face things as we found them. So much for our hopes, our expectations, our dreams, our convictions, above all, our enthusiasm!

Tortured by these questions and these doubts, Nestrov and I were sorely tempted to find some way to leave Russia and return to Poland, where we could at least act as priests again, even if with difficulty in an occupied country. The people there surely needed us in times of persecution; the people there would come to us if they knew we were available. We could serve the Church there, we could do nothing here. This whole Russian venture seemed now to have been a mistake, an ill-conceived missionary effort based on hopes and dreams rather than on hard facts, a plan born of insufficient information and misinformation.

That was the temptation that Father Nestrov and I faced at Teplaya-Gora. And though our situation may have been somewhat unique, the temptation itself was not. It is the same temptation faced by everyone who has followed a call and found that the realities of life were nothing like the expectations he had in the first flush of his vision and his enthusiasm. It is the temptation that comes to anyone, for example, who has entered religious life with a burning desire to serve God and him alone, only to find that the day-to-day life in religion is humdrum and pedestrian, equally as filled with moments of human misunderstanding, daily routines, and distractions as the secular life he left behind in the world. It is the same temptation faced by young couples in marriage, when the honeymoon is over, and they must face a seemingly endless future of living together and scratching out an existence in the same old place and the same old way. It is the temptation to say: "This life is not what I thought it would be. This is not what I bargained for. It is not at all what I wanted, either. If I had known it would be like this, I would never have made this choice, I would never have made this promise. You must forgive me, God, but I want to go back. You cannot hold me to a promise made in ignorance; you cannot expect me to keep a covenant based on faith without any previous knowledge of the true facts of life. It is not fair. I never thought it would be like this. I simply cannot stand it, and I will not stay. I will not serve."

It is a temptation that comes to every man and woman, sometimes daily. That it should have come to Nestrov and me in the terrible surroundings of Teplaya-Gora is not surprising in retrospect, and yet we almost gave in to it. We spoke of finding ways to return to Lvov. We argued that it was only right to report to our superiors, that we should tell them of the true circumstances in the Urals before any more men were sent on such a mission. We continued our work in the lumber camps, looking always for a chance to leave, and resorted to prayer to sustain us in the meantime.

Our one spiritual consolation was the Mass. Occasionally, we were able to get away, just the two of us, into the forest and there celebrate a Mass in secret. We wore no vestments, the stump of a tree served as our altar, and we had to be constantly on guard against discovery. In some ways, this need for secrecy in celebrating the sacrifice of the Mass only served to emphasize the difficulties we had encountered, the near impossibility of ever doing what we had come to do for the people to whom we had hoped to minister. Yet the Mass gave us strength. We preached little homilies after the Gospel, first Father Nestrov and then I. It was amazing how impressive the Gospel message could be in such circumstances; our spirits would seem to drink in the words, savor them, and feel the divine power in them. And, at the moment of Consecration, God became present in a new way in Teplaya-Gora. He was there, in answer to our petitions, where the sacrifice of Calvary had never been celebrated before. In that sacrament we could offer up all our sacrifices with his, could ask his blessing on those for whom we labored and prayed in secret, for those who themselves were perhaps praying in secret, but who couldn't worship him publicly. Those were my most consoling thoughts, my happiest moments, in what had turned out to be almost a non-apostolate at Teplaya-Gora. The consolation of that sacrifice, that offering, would stay with me as we returned home through the darkness and silence of the forest.

And then one day, together, it dawned on us. God granted us the grace to see the solution to our dilemma, the answer to our temptation. It was the grace quite simply to look at our situation from his viewpoint rather than from ours. It was the grace not to judge our efforts by human standards, or by what we ourselves wanted or expected to happen, but rather according to God's design. It was the grace to understand that our dilemma, our temptation, was of our own making and existed only in our minds; it did not and could not coincide with the real world ordained by God and governed ultimately by his will.

St. Ignatius puts it starkly and forthrightly in his First Principle

and Foundation: "Man is created to praise, reverence, and serve
God Our Lord, and by this means to save his soul. The other
things on the face of the earth are created for man to help him in
attaining the end for which he is created. Hence, man is to make
use of them insofar as they help him in the attainment of his end,
and he must rid himself of them insofar as they prove a hindrance
to him. Therefore, we must make ourselves indifferent to all
created things." Ignatius calls that the Principle and Foundation of
his Spiritual Exercises, but it is also the most fundamental truth of
man's existence and God's providence. Those four sentences put it
as plainly and simply as it can be put. How often had Nestrov and
I heard those words, read those statements, prayed and meditated
over them? And yet, under the pressure of circumstances at Teplaya-
Gora, we had forgotten them. We had accepted them as abstract
principles of the spiritual life, but they had not become part of our
daily lives. At least they had not so far been operative in our
approach to life and our dilemma at Teplaya-Gora.

If they had been, we would have understood much earlier that
our sole purpose at Teplaya-Gora—as indeed in our whole lives—
was to do the will of God. Not the will of God as we might wish
it, or as we might have envisioned it, or as we thought in our poor
human wisdom it ought to be. But rather the will of God as God
envisioned it and revealed it to us each day in the created situations with which he presented us. His will for us was the twenty-
four hours of each day: the people, the places, the circumstances
he set before us in that time. Those were the things God knew
were important to him and to us *at that moment,* and those were
the things upon which he wanted us to act, not out of any abstract
principle or out of any subjective desire to "do the will of God".
No, these things, the twenty-four hours of this day, were his will;
we had to learn to recognize his will in the reality of the situation
and to act accordingly. We had to learn to look at our daily lives,
at everything that crossed our path each day, with the eyes of
God; learning to see his estimate of things, places, and above all
people, recognizing that he had a goal and a purpose in bringing
us into contact with these things and these people, and striving
always to do that will—his will—every hour of every day in the

situations in which he had placed us. For to what other purpose had we been created? For what other reason had he so arranged it that we should be here, now, this hour, among these people? To what other end had he ordained our being here, if not to see his will in these situations and to strive to do always what he wanted, the way he wanted it, as he would have done it, for his sake, that he might have the fruit and the glory?

Our dilemma at Teplaya-Gora came from our frustration at not being able to do what we thought the will of God ought to be in this situation, at our inability to work as we thought God would surely want us to work, instead of accepting the situation itself as his will. It is a mistake easily made by every man, saint or scholar, Church leader or day laborer. Ultimately, we come to expect God to accept *our* understanding of what his will ought to be and to help us fulfill *that,* instead of learning to see and accept his will in the real situations in which he places us daily. The simple soul who each day makes a morning offering of "all the prayers, works, joys, and sufferings of this day"—and who then acts upon it by accepting unquestioningly and responding lovingly to all the situations of the day as truly sent by God—has perceived with an almost childlike faith the profound truth about the will of God. To predict what God's will is going to be, to rationalize about what his will must be, is at once a work of human folly and yet the subtlest of all temptations. The plain and simple truth is that his will is what he actually wills to send us each day, in the way of circumstances, places, people, and problems. The trick is to learn to see that—not just in theory, or not just occasionally in a flash of insight granted by God's grace, but every day. Each of us has no need to wonder about what God's will must be for us; his will for us is clearly revealed in every situation of every day, if only we could learn to view all things as he sees them and sends them to us.

The temptation is to overlook these things as God's will. The temptation is to look beyond these things, precisely because they are so constant, so petty, so humdrum and routine, and to seek to discover instead some other and nobler "will of God" in the abstract that better fits *our* notion of what his will should be. And that was our temptation at Teplaya-Gora, just as it is the temptation faced by everyone who suddenly discovers that life is not what he expected it to be. The answer lies in understanding that it is these things—and these things alone, here and now, at this moment—that truly constitute the will of God. The challenge lies in learning to accept this truth and act upon it, every moment of every day. The trouble is that like all great truths it seems too simple. It is there before our noses all the time, while we look elsewhere for more subtle answers. It bears the hallmark of all divine truths, simplicity, and yet it is precisely because it seems so simple that we are prone to overlook it or ignore it in our daily lives.

Like every divine truth, moreover, it is far from simple of execution. Its very simplicity renders it at once almost impossible not just of credibility but of human achievement, for our poor human nature is too easily distracted. The very circumstances of our lives—so constant and so humdrum and routine, and yet the things that truly constitute the will of God for us each day—are also the very things that serve so to distract us, precisely because we are so involved in them, and cause us to lose sight, however momentarily, of this great truth. And yet to grasp this divine truth, simple as it sounds, and work at it, to face each moment of every day in the light of its inspiration, to attempt insofar as we can to recall it in every situation and circumstance of our daily lives, to labor day in and day out to make it the sole principle by which our every action is guided and toward which we aim, is to come to know at last true joy and peace of heart, secure in the knowledge we are attempting always and in everything to do God's will, the only purpose ultimately for which we exist, the end for which alone we were created. There is no greater security a man could ask, no greater serenity a man can know.

Chapter Four

ARREST AND IMPRISONMENT

The German Army launched its blitzkrieg into Russia on June 22, 1941; the Soviet Union immediately declared a state of war. That same night, at three o'clock in the morning, the secret police came to our barracks at Teplaya-Gora. Father Nestrov and I, along with our roommates Fuchs, Valery, and Janocz were arrested at gunpoint as German spies. Hundreds of others were arrested in the lumber camp that night. We were detained overnight in Chusovoy and then taken by train, under heavy guard, to the *oblast* (district) prison at Perm. There I was photographed—front and profile, standard prison procedure—had my hair clipped off, was deloused, and put into a large cell, perhaps thirty by thirty feet. It held five people when I entered in the morning; by nightfall, it was crowded with more than a hundred. Threatened by the German invasion, the Soviets seemed to be arresting anyone of whom they had the slightest suspicion. There were teachers, ordinary workers, minor officials in the government, lawyers, a few soldiers—just about anyone, it seemed, who might be considered a bad security risk.

Father Nestrov and I had always known that we might one day be arrested; we had on occasion discussed the notion of arrest as a possibility. When our arrest became a reality, however, it happened so quickly that it all seemed unreal. I could not believe it was actually happening to me. I was in a daze, disoriented. My mind simply could not adjust itself to all that was happening— especially the total loss of freedom and the immediate deprivation of all rights or the possibility of any recourse. There was no way to argue, no way to plead innocence, no way to tell anyone it was all a mistake. The secret police had their orders; they were men with a job to do. They simply rounded us up like so many head of cattle. They wanted to hear no protests, they were in no mood for arguments, and they shunted aside all questions of innocence or rights, brusquely and completely, by ignoring them.

That experience is something you cannot describe adequately. Anyone who has ever been arrested by mistake or held overnight in jail will know the feeling, but I cannot find words to convey fully the shock, both emotional and physical, that comes over you in such an experience. Helplessness may be the closest one-word description of that feeling, and yet how pale and inadequate it seems, to express the reality. You feel completely cut off from everything and everyone who might conceivably help you, unable to make a move to help yourself and powerless to get in touch immediately with anyone who might help, totally at the mercy of those who have you in custody, not free to go anywhere or take any action unless they allow it. It is as if an iron door has slammed on the world you know and can operate in, and you have entered a totally new universe with its own set of rules and powers and boundaries. Those who give the orders do not have to listen, nor do they ever seem to have to make an accounting to anyone. You, on the other hand, are helpless to say or do anything that might affect your plight for the better.

Helplessness is the word. If I had felt frustrated at Teplaya-Gora because I could not work among the people the way I had hoped, that feeling of frustration was as nothing compared to this sinking feeling of helplessness and powerlessness. Even when I recovered somewhat from the shock that followed on the suddenness of my arrest, I could not overcome the shock occasioned by the total loss of freedom and the sense of complete control held by someone else over my every action, my every liberty, my every need. All prisons must create in their inmates, especially in new inmates, this feeling of absolute frustration and total helplessness. They cannot help but be dehumanizing to some extent, debilitating the mind, degrading the person. But a Soviet prison during wartime, the Soviet prisons run by Stalin's secret police, were especially so. People could disappear into those prisons and never be heard of again. Prisoners could be and were shot. Control by authorities was absolute; the prisoners' lack of recourse was complete. Fear and terror were the favorite weapons of the secret police. If their power of life and death over prisoners was not total and complete in actuality, it surely seemed so to the prisoners and the general population at the time. A concern for sheer survival reduced prisoners under these conditions to a state of docility and servility that was truly inhuman.

The physical conditions, too, were inhuman. The cells were so badly overcrowded there was scarcely room to move. There was no running water, slop buckets served as toilets. The windows were covered by metal shutters, so there was little light and less fresh air. We were filthy, we had no such thing as a change of clothes, we slept on the unwashed floor with insects crawling over us. The air was always foul, and you could not get the reek of that nauseating stench out of your nostrils. You simply had to learn to ignore it as best you could.

It was all so degrading, so humiliating, that some men just ceased to think of themselves as men. And gnawing at the mind through it all was that feeling of helplessness and injustice. Most of the men in our cell were political prisoners like myself; they really had no idea of why they were in prison. Few could honestly accuse themselves of any deliberate transgression against the state. Many of them tried to console themselves at first by believing that their arrest was a mistake, that somebody soon would discover the blunder and set them free. They were quickly disillusioned, bitter, raging with injustice. Yet what could they do, what recourse did they have? Their rights were totally disregarded, they were considered traitors or worse, they were constantly under threat of being shot. There was nowhere to turn for help; indeed, every protest was considered a new transgression, a new violation, a new betrayal of confidence in "the system".

Beyond all this misery we shared in common, there was one final humiliation I alone had to bear. In discussing with others the various reasons for our arrests, I made no secret of my thought that one of the reasons, surely, for my arrest was the fact I was a priest. If I thought this revelation might serve to emphasize my innocence, or give my fellow prisoners a greater sense of trust and confidence in me, or even give me an opportunity to serve them better or console them in their anguish, I was in for a rude awakening. I was treated instead with contempt. Apparently the many years of Soviet propaganda had had some effect. I was shocked to learn that many of my fellow prisoners looked on priests as parasites in society, living a life of ease paid for by the pennies of poor old women, or as immoral men given to drinking, women chasers or perverts. The more educated prisoners or minor party officials had acquired a distorted image of the Church from communist tracts in which the political, social, and human aspects of the Church were described with all their errors, shortcomings, abuses, and injustices. A priest to them, at best, meant a man out of step and out of place in a socialist society; at worst, he was a dupe in the employ of a Church that was itself a willing tool of capitalism.

I was stunned at the depth of feeling and prejudice against the Church that came spilling out. The more so under the circumstances. Most of us in this cell were political prisoners, nearly all of us unjustly suspected or accused of things we never did and yet not given an opportunity to answer the charges or to prove our innocence. We shared a common grievance and a common sense of personal anguish, outrage, humiliation, and helplessness. There was at least a minimal sense of camaraderie among the political prisoners in the cell, a certain companionship in misery. But not for me when it became known I was a priest. I was cursed at; I was shunned; I was looked down upon and despised. Against the background of my Polish Catholic upbringing, where a priest was always treated as someone special whether you liked him as a person or not, this reaction to a priest on the part of my fellow prisoners made me by turns angry and bewildered. I was at a loss to understand it and furious at the added injustice of this stupid, blind prejudice. I was very nearly reduced to tears. It all seemed so totally unfair, so completely unjust, so degrading, so humiliating. Just as we all felt powerless to defend ourselves in the prison system itself, so on this level too I found I was not even able to explain myself or defend myself. Nobody would listen, very few in fact would even talk to me. In the words of Isaiah, I felt "despised and the most abject of men". To both prison officials and fellow prisoners alike, I was a thing of no value; I was worthless. And so, added to the common feeling of helplessness and powerlessness, I suffered the hollow and sickening sense of being useless as well.

There was no one to turn to, no one to talk to, no one from whom I could seek advice or sympathetic understanding, no one to offer me any consolation. I had not seen Father Nestrov since our arrest. The other roommates from the camp who had been arrested with us must all have been in other cells. And so, as I had done in every other crisis, I turned to God in prayer. I sought his help, his sympathy, his consolation. Since I was suffering especially for his sake, since I was despised precisely because I was one of his priests, he could not fail to comfort me when he himself, in his human life, had fitted Isaiah's description of "despised and the most abject of men." He too had sought for someone to comfort him and had found none. Surely he could sympathize with my plight; surely he would comfort and console me.

His way of consoling me, however, as had happened so often in the past, was to increase my self-knowledge and my understanding of both his providence and the mystery of salvation. When I turned to him in prayer in the depths of my humiliation, when I ran to him utterly dejected because I felt useless and despised, the grace I received in return was the light to recognize how large an admixture of self had crept into the picture. I had been humiliated and I was feeling sorry for myself. No one appreciated me as a priest, and I was indulging in self-pity. I was being treated unfairly, unjustly, out of prejudice. There was no one to listen to my sad story and offer me sympathy, so I was feeling sorry for myself. That was really the extent of my "humiliation".

Yes, the physical conditions in this cell were inhuman. Maybe they were even designed to be inhuman, to sap the prisoners' wills, to destroy that one spiritual power that makes men truly men and free and strong. But because the conditions were inhuman was no reason that I, or any other man, had therefore to cease to be human. We were not, and did not have to be, the product of our environment. The conditions were degrading only if we let ourselves become degraded.

As for the humiliation I felt because I did not get the proper respect as a priest of God, was "the servant greater than the master"? Our Lord had said to his disciples, "If they despised me, they will despise you." I had been taught from my youth to respect a priest because he represented God among men. But as a priest I had also come to expect this respect (and even some adulation) from others. How then did I truly think I was following in the footsteps of the Master? If I had been more truly like Christ, should I not have expected rejection and humiliation? Why should I be shocked when it occurred? Should I not rather rejoice that I had been allowed to imitate him more closely?

In how many other ways, too, had I allowed this admixture of self, this luxury of feeling sorry for myself, to cloud my vision and prevent me from seeing the current situation with the eyes of God? No man, no matter what his situation, is ever without value, is ever useless in God's eyes. No situation is ever without its worth and purpose in God's providence. It is a very human temptation to feel frustrated by circumstances, to feel overwhelmed and helpless in the face of the established order—whether that order is an NKVD prison, or the whole Soviet system, or "the status quo", or "city hall", or "the rat race", or the "establishment", or social pressures, or the cultural environment, or the whole, oppressive rotten world! Under the worst imaginable circumstances, a man remains a man with free will and God stands ready to assist him with his grace. Indeed, more than that, God expects him to *act* in these circumstances, this situation, as he would have him act. For these situations, too, these people and places and things, are God's will for him now.

He may not be able to change the "system", any more than I could change conditions in that prison, but he is not for that reason excused from acting at all. Many men feel frustrated, or disappointed, or even defeated, when they find themselves face to face with a situation or an evil they cannot do much about. Poverty, addiction, alcoholism, social injustice, racial discrimination, hatred and bitterness, war, corruption, and the oppressive bureaucracy of every institution—all can serve as a source of bitter frustration and a feeling sometimes of utter hopelessness. But God does not expect a man single-handedly to change the world or overthrow all evil or cure all ills. He does expect him, though, to act as he would have him act in these circumstances ordained by his will and his providence. Nor will God's grace be lacking to help him act.

The sense of hopelessness we all experience in such circumstances really arises from our tendency to inject too much of self into the picture. Doing so, we can easily be overwhelmed by personal feelings of inadequacy or sheer physical powerlessness, by the realization of one man's seeming insignificance in a corrupt world. We tend to concentrate on ourselves, we tend to think of what we can or cannot do, and we forget about God and his will and his providence. Yet God never forgets each individual's significance, his dignity and worth, and the role each has been asked to play in the workings of his providence. To him, each individual is equally important at all times. He cares. But he also expects each man to accept, as from his hands, the daily situations he sends him and to act as he would have him act and gives him the grace to act.

What each man *can* change, first of all, is himself. And each will have—indeed, must have—some influence on the people God brings into his life each day. He is expected, as a Christian, to influence them for good. He may instead influence them for evil, but they will touch his life this day—for God sees to that—and he will therefore have some influence of some kind upon them. He will in some small way at least touch their lives, too, and it is in that touching that God will hold him responsible for the good or ill he does. In that simple truth lies the key to any understanding of the mystery of divine providence and ultimately of each man's salvation.

No, I was not helpless or worthless or useless in that prison at Perm. I was not terribly humiliated because I was rejected as a priest. These men around me were suffering, they needed help. They needed someone to listen to them with sympathy, someone to comfort them, someone to give them courage to carry on. They needed someone who was not feeling sorry for himself but who could truly share in their sorrow. They needed someone who was not looking for consolation but who could console. They needed someone who was not looking for respect and admiration because of what he was but someone who could show them love and respect even if spurned and rejected himself. As Christ had set the example for me, so could I be to them an example of Christian charity and concern. If nothing else, if they insisted upon shunning me, I could at least pray for them and offer up for them to the Father of us all the suffering and anguish that their rejection of me as a priest caused me. Christ had prayed for his persecutors, "Father, forgive them." If I could do nothing else at this moment in the prison at Perm, I could do that.

God does not ask the impossible of any man. He was not asking more of me, really, than he asks of every man, every Christian, each day of his life. He was asking only that I learn to see these suffering men around me, these circumstances in the prison at Perm, as sent from his hand and ordained by his providence. He was asking me to *do* something, as another Christ; to forget about self and feeling sorry for myself, and to act in the situation after the example of Christ himself. He was asking me to forget about my "powerlessness" against the "system", and to look instead to the immediate needs of those around me, this day, in order that I might do everything that it was in my power to do by prayer and example. That was *all* he was asking of me or expecting of me. It was all I had to do, but it was plenty—and it could not be done while I sat feeling sorry for myself. Nor was I powerless to do it, for it was within my power to do it and I could count on his grace to sustain me. And not the least of his graces was the light to see and understand this truth; to see that this day, like all the days of my life, came from his hands and served a purpose in his providence. I had to learn to believe that, no matter what the circumstances, and to act accordingly—with complete trust and confidence in his will, his wisdom, and his grace.

Chapter Five

LUBIANKA

Because I was considered a Vatican spy, a charge I never could get used to taking seriously but which the NKVD seemed to take quite seriously indeed, I was transferred under guard from the oblast prison at Perm to Moscow and the Lubianka Prison. "Lubianka" was a dreaded word then in Russia. The prison on Lubianka Street was spoken of in fearful whispers as the place where the NKVD did its best (or worst) work. Men were broken there in body and spirit. During the days of Stalin's terror before the war, comrades from the highest levels of the party were taken to Lubianka and emerged again for the famous "show trials" as hollow figures of their former selves, their spirits spilled out in the depths of dreaded Lubianka. Others were simply swallowed up into its gates and never emerged again. Tales of terror, torture, and summary execution were recounted as common occurrences at Lubianka. It was not so much the NKVD's maximum security prison as it was their headquarters for maximum mischief. Fortunately, I had heard little of all this when I arrived there after the long train trip from Perm, alone, under guard.

Lubianka had formerly been a hotel. Its cells were still more like hotel rooms than prison cells. They were small but neat, very clean, with a shining wooden floor, and whitewashed walls and ceiling lit by a naked light bulb hanging from the center. There was a regular window in the room, but it was completely barred and covered over with a huge sheet of tin. Only a little bit of sky showed through at the top, where the tin had been tilted away from the window frame to let in light and air. The door was a regular hotel-like door, but iron-sheeted, with a special bolt operated from the outside and a round peephole for the guard to look through that was covered on the outside with a hinged cover so the prisoner could not see out. There was an iron bed in one corner with clean sheets, a blanket, and a pillow. That was the only bit of furniture, except for a *parasha* (a toilet bucket with a lid) in the corner near the door. No table, no chair, nothing to sit on. Only during the hours allowed for sleep could you lie on the bed. Accordingly, prisoners spent their days standing or slouching against the wall or pacing restlessly and endlessly back and forth, up and down the little six-by-ten-foot room.

We were allowed a twenty-minute exercise period in the court-yard of the prison each day if weather permitted, and twice a day there was a trip down the corridors up to the toilet, where we were allowed two minutes to empty the *parasha* and a hurried wash-up at tap faucets. Other than that, our whole universe at Lubianka was that little whitewashed room with its bed, its barred and covered window, and its solidly locked door with that eternal, prying peephole. Anyone who has ever been "cooped up" in a hotel room for any length of time, or confined to a sickroom or hospital room or dormitory room, knows the feelings that such continued isolation in close quarters can produce. But at Lubianka there was no end to it, at least as far as the prisoner could control or foresee. The days seemed to stretch out endlessly, hour after hour, with no variation other than the fact the guard might begin serving meals from one end of the corridor instead of the other and so vary by an hour or more the prisoner's constant craving for food. An hour can seem an eternity in such isolation, and time has little meaning at all after a while. A week was simply seven identical twenty-four-hour days, a month simply a mathematical way of marking four such weeks, thirty such days of sameness.

The world of the solitary confined is a universe of its own. In Lubianka, it was not only a very restricted world but a highly regimented one. There were exact rules and regulations concerning behavior within the cells, or for walking in the corridor, or for the few minutes spent each day in the toilet, or for the time of exercise in the courtyard. Violations of these rules were punished by further limiting the few things left to the prisoner: e.g., the exercise period, or the food at meals. As the days stretched out in an endless string, such rules gave a pattern to living but they also became another source of harassment; they seemed to emphasize over and over again the feeling of confinement and the agonizing lack of any freedom.

And then there was the silence. Whether to enhance the morguelike quiet of Lubianka, or simply for comfort and cleanliness, the guards wore special cloth shoes so you couldn't hear them moving along the corridor until they were practically on top of your door. There was never anyone to talk to; there were few sounds along the corridor except at mealtimes. As a result, prisoners became abnormally sensitive to the slightest sound. You couldn't help straining unconsciously, nearly always, to hear something that would break the total and all-pervading silence that seemed to close in around you and threaten you constantly. The sudden sounds of the guard swinging open the peephole or of a door bolt being crashed back made everyone jumpy. It was a cause almost for terror, and yet the tomblike quiet was constantly terrifying in its own way.

I spent five years in Lubianka, most of it alone in such silence. Occasionally, I was moved from cell to cell; sometimes, for a few days or a few weeks, I shared a cell with somebody else. Yet even that was carefully planned by the NKVD. Cellmates were used, knowingly or unknowingly, to discover if their fellow prisoner would tell them something he had not told the interrogator. It was a trap, and yet the psychological need, bred of prolonged isolation and silence, to talk to a fellow sufferer unceasingly, hour after hour, about everything and anything, was unbearable. There were infrequent and unpredictable sessions with the interrogators, too. They might occur daily for months at a time, and then not again for several months, while the days, the hours, and the minutes of silence and solitary routine stretched out without end. Individual sessions with the interrogator might last a few hours, or go non-stop for twenty-four hours or forty-eight hours or more, with teams of interrogators changing places while the prisoner got no rest, no sleep, no food at all. Yet bad as such sessions were, much as you dreaded the trip down the corridors

and up the stairs to the interrogators' chambers, there were times
in the awful silence of Lubianka and the endless routine of solitary
confinement that you could almost look forward to such a terrible
ordeal out of the sheer need to see another face and have someone
to talk to.

The intolerable conditions, the cramped quarters, and foul air
of the crowded cells at Perm had been horrible at the time, but in
retrospect they seemed in every way preferable to the clean,
whitewashed confined world of solitary in Lubianka. In those
crowded cells, at least, there was always someone to talk to,
someone to share your misery, someone to show sympathy or to
give advice or tell you not to give up, or how to survive. After
you returned from a session with the interrogator at Perm, you
could tell somebody about it, you could rehash it, you could look
together for weak answers or stupid answers, or try to figure out
together what the interrogator had been driving at, what was
behind the particular line of questioning and what sort of an
answer might have gotten you off the hook and satisfied somebody "higher up". There was no such sort of human companionship to sustain you at Lubianka. When you came back from an
interrogation session here, you were on your own. You could
only torture yourself by going over and over the session in your
own mind, wondering whether what you had said was right, or
what you might have done better, agonizing again and again over
every question and every answer. Here there was no relief to be
sought by talking it over with somebody else, by asking advice
(poor as it might prove to be), by sharing experiences and
sympathizing with one another. Solitary confinement, in short,
must be very much like what some theologians paint as the
principal torment of hell: the soul at last recognizing its mistakes
for what they were and condemned forever to the loss of heaven,
constantly tormenting itself with reproaches and tearing itself
apart because it still sees and understands and wants the things it
has lost forever, but knows it is condemned to lose forever because
of its own choices, its own failings, its own mistakes.

The human mind is restless, and it cannot be confined. It will
go on, every waking hour, thinking of something, recalling

something, dreaming of something, or dreading some future happening with present fear and anxiety. You can control this restlessness, you can channel it, but you cannot stop it. And when you are shut off from all outside sources, when you are left alone in silence and solitary confinement with this surging sea of thoughts and memories and questionings and fears that is the human mind, you either learn to control and channel it or you can go mad. Time may seem to stand still, but the human mind is never quiet. An hour can become an eternity, but the human mind can fill every second of it with a million thoughts and a million questions and a million fears. Again and again, in the eternal hours of Lubianka, I had nothing to do but go over my past life and future fears with ample time for reflection and questioning. But above all I prayed.

At first I found it difficult to believe that the Soviets could take seriously the charges on which I was being held and interrogated. I could tell from their questions that they knew everything about me and everything I had done. Beyond that, I was the possessor of no terrible secrets. I considered my case a simple one and not really worth all the attention they were giving to it. And I believed that they would soon see it the same way. I was hardly worth all their effort, and nothing I had done was deserving of death. Since I believed that, I was at first rather untroubled. The interrogations were annoying and sometimes painful, but they didn't really disturb me in the beginning. I really felt that, sooner or later, the "higher-ups" would realize what I already knew – that I wasn't worth bothering about. My conscience was clear, so my morale in the beginning stood firm and high.

For that matter, I had a great deal of confidence in myself. I hardly thought the interrogators would get me to admit to something I hadn't done just to prove their case; I was naturally stubborn and strong-willed and, besides, I had spent a great part of my life developing willpower and training the will. I rather prided myself on that and felt I could probably hold my own with any interrogator. So again, since I knew I hadn't done anything greatly wrong and felt confident that nobody could make me admit to something I hadn't done, I remained at first in pretty good spirits and expected the NKVD soon to discover its own mistake in treating me as someone special.

After a few sessions of the Lubianka interrogations, however, and some seemingly endless months in solitary, I began to have second thoughts. It dawned on me that the NKVD could wipe out its mistake, if I were nobody special, by a simple order of execution. There wouldn't be any lawyers, there wouldn't be any trial, and there wouldn't be any appeal. The Soviet Union was at war. Thousands were dying every day, and spies and traitors were shot with very few questions asked. Interrogators had put it just that bluntly. I had failed by then to convince them of either my innocence or my insignificance, so I was also beginning to doubt my own powers in the face of the full might and methods of the NKVD. I never quite believed that I would actually be shot, but the doubt and the fear began to filter into my self-confidence. And the agonizing afterthoughts that filled the hours in my silent cell after each period of interrogation, the constant reviewing of questions and answers, the agony of going over and over the same ground again and again, began to have their effect and to eat away at my morale. It was then, especially, that I turned to prayer.

Very early in my stay at Lubianka, as the endless tedium of solitary confinement began to get to me, I decided to arrange some order and division into the day. I made up for myself what we used to call in the Jesuit houses at home a "daily order". As soon as we were awakened in the morning, I would say the Morning Offering; then, after the morning trip to the toilet and wash-up, I would put in a solid hour of meditation. The 5:30 A.M. rising hour and seven o'clock breakfast in Lubianka were almost identical to the daily order in most of the Jesuit houses I had lived in, so the days began to fall into a pattern for me again.

After breakfast, I would say Mass by heart—that is, I would say all the prayers, for of course I had no way actually to celebrate the Holy Sacrifice. I said the Angelus morning, noon, and night as the Kremlin clock tolled the hours over Red Square a few blocks from Lubianka Street. At noon, I would make an examination of conscience as suggested by St. Ignatius in his Spiritual Exercises. I would make another *examen* before going to bed at night, and also prepare the points for my next morning's meditation. Each afternoon, I said three rosaries—one in Polish, one in Latin, and one in Russian—as a substitute for my breviary.

Occasionally, too, I would chant hymns in Polish or Latin or English, the hymns I could remember from my boyhood days or from the years of Jesuit training, or the chants I had worked so hard to learn from the Russian liturgy during my years at the Russicum in Rome. Sometimes I would spend hours trying to remember a line that slipped my memory, going over it time and again until it sounded right. Sometimes I think it became more a mental exercise than a prayer; it was a way of passing time, and time was the one thing I had plenty of. "*Qui cantat bis orat* [He who chants, prays twice]" is an old monastic axiom. I would hesitate to argue that God was doubly pleased with my hymn singing in Lubianka, but I'm sure he must have understood.

Being human, I made the same mistakes in prayer every human being makes. I prayed for the conversion of my interrogators, for example, but none of them ever showed the slightest sign of conversion. I also prayed hard for more food. Prison food was always poor and inadequate, but the wartime rationing in Lubianka resulted in a more meager and more miserable portion even than normal. I was constantly hungry, so much so that my first thought upon finishing the last bit of thin soup or the last drop of hot water at any meal would always be a reckoning of how long it would be to the next meal. There was no way not to think such thoughts in the extreme hunger we suffered in those days; the bodily craving for more food generated by each minimal meal simply drove all other thoughts out of mind for a while. And the actual pangs of hunger, when they returned, would be so extreme that you could not believe any other pain or sufferings could ever equal that torment. Frankly, thoughts of suicide would actually force themselves into your consciousness as a way to end that awful agony. And some men, I have heard, actually did choose that form of death rather than the torturously slow death by starvation. Nevertheless, pray as I might, I never received an extra portion of food or cup of hot water.

The fasts, abstinences, and self-imposed penances I had practiced in the past made it somewhat easier, I guess, to bear the ordeals of hunger we endured during those prison years. At least for me the experience was not new, except in its intensity. And I learned soon enough that prayer does not take away bodily pain or mental anguish. Nevertheless, it does provide a certain moral strength to bear the burden patiently. Certainly, it was prayer that helped me through every crisis.

Gradually, too, I learned to purify my prayer and remove from it the elements of self-seeking. I learned to pray for my interrogators, not so they would see things my way or come to the truth so that my ordeal would end, but because they, too, were children of God and human beings in need of his blessing and his daily grace. I learned to stop asking for more bread for myself, and instead to offer up my sufferings, the pains of hunger that I felt, for the many others in the world and in Russia at that time who were enduring similar agony and even greater suffering. I tried very hard not to worry about what tomorrow would bring, what I should eat, or what I should wear, but rather to seek the kingdom of God and his justice, his will for me and for all mankind.

"Thy will be done." That was the key, but only slowly did I come to experience how perfect a prayer is the Our Father, the Lord's Prayer. "Lord, teach us how to pray", the disciples had said, and in his answer the Lord had explained the whole theology of prayer in the most simple terms, exhaustive in its content and yet intended for the use of all men without distinction. The human mind could not elaborate a better pattern in prayer than the one the Lord himself gave us.

He begins by placing us in the presence of God. God the almighty, who has created all things out of nothingness and keeps them in existence lest they return to nothingness, who rules all things and governs all things in the heavens and on earth according to the designs of his own providence. And yet this same all-powerful God is our Father, who cherishes us and looks after us as his sons, who provides for us in his own loving kindness, guides us in his wisdom, who watches over us daily to shelter us from harm, to provide us food, to receive us back with open arms when we, like the prodigal, have wasted our inheritance. Even as a father guards his children, he guards us from evil—because evil does exist in the world. And just as he can find it in his Father's heart to pardon us, he expects us to imitate him in pardoning his other sons, our brothers, no matter what their offenses.

The Our Father is a prayer of praise and thanksgiving, a prayer of petition and of reparation. It encompasses in its short and simple phrases every relation between man and his Creator, between us and our loving, heavenly Father. It is a prayer for all times, for every occasion. It is at once the most simple of prayers and the most profound. One could meditate continuously on each word and phrase of that formula and never fully exhaust its riches. If one could only translate each of its phrases into the actions of his daily life, then he would indeed be perfect as his heavenly Father clearly wishes him to be. Truly, the Lord's Prayer is the beginning and end of all prayers, the key to every other form of prayer.

If we could constantly live in the realization that we are sons of a heavenly Father, that we are always in his sight and play in his creation, then all our thoughts and our every action would be a prayer. For we would be constantly turning to him, aware of him, questioning him, thanking him, asking his help, or begging his pardon when we have fallen. And every true prayer begins precisely here: placing oneself in the presence of God. It is a phrase all spiritual writers use, it is a concept each may visualize in his own way, but the realization of it in practice is sometimes most difficult to achieve. Words do not make a prayer, even the words of the Our Father taught us by our Lord himself, or the words of any other familiar prayer made easy by constant repetition. There is no formula that works of itself, no magic charm that must automatically be heard by God and produce its effect. Prayer, true prayer, is a communication—and it occurs only when two people, two minds, are truly present to each other in some way. So in prayer we must do more than merely visualize God as present as some sort of father figure. His fictionalized presence will not do; his imaginative presence will not do. By faith we know that God is present everywhere and is always present to us if we but turn to him. So it is we who must put ourselves in God's presence, we who must turn to him in faith, we who must leap beyond an image to the belief—indeed the realization—that we are in the presence of a loving Father who stands always ready to listen to our childish stories and to answer to our childlike trust.

It sounds so easy when spiritual writers describe it or novice masters speak of it. In fact, on those rare occasions when it does happen, prayer *is* easy. Conversation with God comes easily whenever God is felt—there are no other words to describe the experience—to be present to the soul. But the human mind is so easily distracted. What is more, it is so easily deceived. It can say the proper words and utter pious formulas as easily as a dog can "speak" for its supper. It has learned what to say, and it will say the proper formula upon the proper cue. Yet such rote formulas are, in and of themselves, no more prayers than are the poor dog's barkings truly speech. God may hear and understand, as we may hear and feed the dog; some minimal communication has been achieved and no effort goes unrewarded with the Lord. But we have not, for all that, truly learned how to pray.

Real prayer occurs, as I have said, when at last we find ourselves in the presence of God. Then every thought becomes the father to a prayer, and words quite often are superfluous. Such prayer is all-absorbing. Once you have experienced it, you can never forget the experience. But I am not speaking here of some great mystical grace. I am speaking only of a conversation with God, the spontaneous outpouring of a soul that has come to realize—however fleetingly—that it is standing at the knee of a loving and providing Father. Thoughts of praise and of thanksgiving spontaneously arise, as well as questions and petitions and thoughts of friends and their needs, mingled with trusting confessions of failure and simple promises to follow in the future only what he would have us do.

Sometimes, by God's grace, such a moment of insight and of prayer occurs almost unexpectedly. But for the most part, prayer demands an effort on our part. We must learn, even as Christ himself did, to draw apart from the circumstances that surround us if we wish to be alone with the Father. In the desert, in the mountains, in the fields, he simply retired, leaving his apostles and disciples and the crowds that followed him, in order to pray to the

Father. And for us, especially, it is easier to find ourselves alone with the Father if we can be physically alone, if we can retire to a place of quiet where we can collect our thoughts.

Because the restless human mind, our chief instrument in all human communications, is also our chief stumbling block to prayer. It seems by nature bent upon distraction rather than on recollection. It prefers to be free, to wander ceaselessly, to seize on each new idea and explore its every direction rather than to fashion its attention upon one direction and remain pinned down. It wants to be forever occupied, constantly at work, worrying, remembering, planning and scheming, preventing and arguing, searching and questioning—even, in our attempts to pray, taking to itself God's part and answering our every petition, carrying on by itself all sides of our attempt at a divine conversation. Or it will flare up with pride, impatience, ill feeling, bitterness, or hate when least we want it to; it will feel injured or offended, guilty or discouraged, just when we have almost reached our goal. Sometimes, indeed very often, the time we have set aside for prayer passes simply in a struggle to control our restless mind, collect our thoughts, and focus our attention upon God. And it is helpful and consoling on such occasions to remember two things: (1) that God himself has initiated this conversation by inspiring us to set aside the time for prayer; and (2) that he appreciates our efforts to respond, and he blesses them.

Posture, like verbal formulas, is not essential to prayer. Perseverance is. Kneeling is not necessarily more conducive to prayer than sitting, nor is standing necessarily better than lying down. Yet mortal man is a peculiar thing made up of body and soul; so our efforts to control the mind can often be connected with an effort at bodily control. Relax the body and the mind goes running off to recreation. We are creatures of habit, and we can sometimes help ourselves achieve a sort of self-control that leads more readily to recollection by taking up a posture we traditionally associate with prayer. Such an effort, moreover, such perseverance is an earnest of our desire to respond to God's promptings and to do his will. An attitude of readiness to try over and over again in our quest to find God and his will in prayer is itself a grace and a blessing of major consequence. What other purpose has man in life but to do God's will? And every effort, at any moment, to follow the promptings of his will is itself both a grace and a blessing of no small consequence.

If we could achieve union with God in prayer, we would then see his will quite clearly and desire nothing but to conform our will to his. So there is truth in the realization that even our most unsuccessful efforts to achieve union with God in prayer are nevertheless an effort to respond to his inspiration and his grace to pray. They are efforts, therefore, to conform our will to his and do his bidding. And perseverance in such efforts is, at the very least, practice in the habit of finding the will of God at all times and in everything.

Lubianka, in many ways, was a school of prayer for me. I was alone, but I did not therefore find it so much easier to pray. Though I was shut away in solitary confinement from the ordinary sights and sounds we think of and spiritual writers speak of as "distractions", it was impossible to confine my mind and keep it recollected. I learned to pray there quite simply as everyone must learn to pray. Weak from hunger, weary and pained after long hours of interrogations, distracted by doubts and growing fears for the future, overcome by anxieties and the abnormal sensitivities induced by constant separation and loneliness, I had to learn to turn to God as best I could and when I could. I had to learn to find him in the midst of trials as well as nerve-racking silences, to discover him and find his will behind all these happenings, to see his hand in all the past experiences of my life, to praise and thank him and ask his blessing on all those faces that crowded to memory (when there was no face to be seen each day except those of my guards), to ask his pardon for my many failures then and now in the interrogations, to promise pardon and to seek to forgive those I sometimes felt were persecuting me, and to ask at every moment his constant, fatherly protection against the evils that seemed to surround me on all sides. "Lord, teach us to pray", the disciples had asked. "He said to them, 'This is how you should pray: Our Father . . .' "

Chapter Six

THE INTERROGATIONS

"And when they bring you to trial and deliver you up, do not be anxious beforehand what you are to say; but say whatever is given you in that hour, for it is not you who speak, but the Holy Spirit." How often did those words run through my mind during the course of my interrogations by the NKVD in Lubianka. Or those other words as recorded by Luke: "Resolve in your heart not to meditate beforehand how to answer, for I will give you a mouth and wisdom which none of your adversaries will be able to withstand or contradict." How often I would have loved to have put down an interrogator with a brilliant remark, an unanswerable argument! Yet it never seemed to work that way.

When I was first summoned for interrogation, I felt completely at ease and confident. I knew the charge of espionage for the Vatican, under which I was being held and because of which I had been brought all the way to Moscow and to Lubianka, was totally false and obviously (I thought) absurd. There was no way I could take such a farfetched charge seriously, and I was certain the NKVD "higher-ups" would be equally unable to take it seriously once they dug into my case and learned the facts. On that score, I was in for a rude awakening. I still don't know whether they seriously believed the charge; perhaps someone "higher up" found it impossible or dangerous to admit that all this trouble had been taken over a nobody and so my interrogators were instructed to prove there had been no mistake. Whatever the reason, they hammered away in deadly earnest to get me to admit to the charge, fantastic as it seemed to me. They were relentless, and they were thorough, and they were good at their trade.

Once the interrogations started at Lubianka after the initial
period of solitary confinement, they went on almost without
letup. Sessions might last for days at a time. All-night sessions,
though, were the usual routine; for some reason they seemingly
were preferred to day interviews. I had a number of interrogators,
who employed a variety of methods. They could be by turns
friendly or hostile, charming or vituperative, angry or dispassionate,
threatening or the voice of sweet reason itself. But their goal was
always the same.

As the interrogations progressed, a set pattern of questions
taken from a printed form lying on the desk were asked of me
over and over again. The interrogator wrote down on big sheets
of paper every answer I gave. Quite often, he seemed to pay little
attention to what I actually said in reply. He wrote continuously,
probably because it was expected of him, and seemed to make
little effort at all really to understand what I was trying to say or
explain. From time to time, the interrogator would sit back in his
chair and read me what he had written. He would ask me if it was
substantially correct. I would try to point out to him how he had
simply twisted the meaning of any factual content to make it
accord with a preconceived and prejudged pattern; most of it was
even couched in catch phrases. My presence among the workers at
Teplaya-Gora, for example, was written up as if I were an outside
agitator come to excite the masses to revolt against the regime and
system.

I tried in the beginning to argue about such things, or to get
the interrogator to change what he had written. If he bothered to
take note of my complaint at all, the interrogator quite generally
replied that he had written the facts as they appeared in the eyes of
Soviet law. The Soviet Constitution allowed the practice of religion on an individual basis, but it forbade the preaching of
religion. And the provision was obviously a wise one, for under
the pretext of teaching religion the Church was actually teaching
hatred of communism; the statements of the Popes on communism
were clear enough evidence of that. He was not there, however,
to argue the point. His job was not to discover whether I was
involved in some plot against the government—my presence in

the country as a foreign priest was evidence enough to put that point beyond question—but to discover all the details of the plot, including others who might have been involved, how it was financed, the means to be employed, and any organizations that might be conspiring with me. Finally, he would accuse me of holding back information from him and suggest that we get down to business.

After I had been over the same questions and the same answers a number of times with a number of interrogators, I simply gave up arguing. I concentrated instead on trying always to give the same answer, for the least little variation on my part would be treated as a slip, a weak point in my story that should be attacked and explored to catch me in a lie or contradiction. And yet if I repeated exactly the same story time after time, gave the same biographical details and chronological sequences, the interrogator might get furious. He would take the very sameness of the answers as proof that they must be part of some carefully memorized lie.

As the months of interrogations lengthened, my original naïve optimism and self-confidence gave way to resentment and repugnance. It became almost unbearable for me to face another session. When called by the guard for another trip along the dimly lit corridors to the interrogators' offices, the sense of revulsion would be so strong that a physical tremor would shake my whole body. It was something beyond my control, and no effort on my part would prevent it. But worst of all, perhaps, I began to give up. I was tired of trying to correct the misinterpretations put upon every action of mine; I just became indifferent to what the interrogator said or wrote. It just seemed so useless to make the attempt any more. I simply shrugged off any more attempts and confined myself wherever possible to yes or no answers, or to a noncommittal "I don't know."

The law provided a month's time for the investigation of a case. My case entered its twelfth month and the interrogations still continued. My patience and my self-confidence, even my innate stubbornness, were gradually wearing away. I was tired of the struggle, I was tired of fighting, but above all I was tired of second-guessing myself in the silence of solitary confinement after the interrogation sessions, tired of the doubts, fears, and the constant anxiety and strain. The last interrogator seemed a reasonable man, soft-spoken and humane. He seemed to understand how anxious I was to end this constant questioning; he suggested we could put an end to it if I would only cooperate and tell the whole truth. He spoke of getting it over with, of getting out of Lubianka and of solitary. That thought alone, the notion of being with people again, was enough to catch me off balance. I really didn't care any more what would ultimately happen to me. I just wanted to get all this rigamarole over with, the sooner the better. "Of course I'll tell the truth", I said, "and cooperate with you." I didn't mean that I was going to tell any lies or agree to anything I hadn't agreed to before; but I wasn't going to fight, either, the interpretation that might be put on the facts I admitted to.

Too late, of course, I realized the mistake I was making. I realized as well the motives prompting my actions, the mental fatigue and the frustration, the desire to be rid at last of the physical and mental strain of both the interrogations and the isolation. Accordingly, as we went over the questions together for the last time, I tried to change course once again. I tried to retreat once more to the high ground I had held so painfully and so stubbornly for so many months. But my gentle, courteous interrogator pressed home his advantage. He seemed so hurt, perhaps annoyed, at the "distinctions" I wanted to make, the "clarifications" I tried to offer. He ignored them, he changed nothing, but he reminded me gently that at this rate the process would never end. I gave up. I convinced myself that my efforts were useless and I let the process roll on with a shrug. After all, I said to myself, what does it really matter? What difference can it possibly make to anyone except to me—and I simply wanted out. I convinced myself that, for my part, I had told only the truth and continued to tell only the truth. All the rest mattered little, except that it would soon end.

Once I had taken that basic decision, it was surprising how easy everything became. If I had any nagging doubts at all, it was about what would happen to me after Lubianka. Come what may, however, this ordeal would soon be over. The end was in sight.

The feeling of relief, of release from tension and from struggling, permeated every other thought. I would have to let tomorrow take care of itself.

Tomorrow came soon enough. The interrogator told me to get ready for my final session. He explained that I would have to sign the documents he had written. I would be expected to read and sign each page of the collected material. He warned me that this was one of the most important steps in the whole process. I don't know why, but I had not really expected that. Now I found myself trapped, and I passed the night in new mental anguish and agony. I resented the seeming kindness and gentleness of the interrogator that had led me so sweetly to this moment. I wished I could take back again that promise to cooperate and the sessions that had followed. Now what could I do? Refuse to sign the documents? And then what? This was the critical hour, if ever, for the Holy Spirit to intervene and protect me and protect the Church. It was now or never. Martyrdom, perhaps, or capitulation.

Still tormented by these thoughts, I was summoned next morning to the interrogator's office. He handed me the volume of materials and asked me to read and sign each page. It was the moment of decision, but I stalled for time. I began to read the materials with growing resentment and incredulity. It seemed incredible that I had ever agreed to go along with this! I continued to read, but I signed nothing. I tried to think, only to discover that somehow my mind had stopped functioning. All I saw before me was a blank. I tried to ask the Holy Spirit to prompt me to say something to the interrogator, to give me the words of wisdom that would startle the interrogator and persuade him now, at this eleventh hour, to believe me and to change the charges brought against me. I prayed for the Spirit to move me—and I felt nothing.

Feeling abandoned by God, I knew I must do something. I wanted to throw that volume on the table and tell the interrogator right out that I would not sign a page of it. Fear stopped me. I struggled with myself. I badly wanted to show him who he was dealing with: not a weakling, or an intimidated priest afraid to stand up for his rights, or an ignoramus who didn't know what was going on. I wanted to speak out and end the deal right then and there. Indeed, the words I wanted so vehemently to blurt out were on the tip of my tongue. I raised my head slowly and looked at the interrogator, who was busy with some other papers. The words "I won't sign", however, never came. I was afraid, and I was angry at myself for being afraid. I made a strenuous effort to overpower the fear afflicting me, but succeeded only in being overcome by it. I was disgusted with myself, terribly upset. I lowered my head again slowly in confusion and pretended to be reading.

But the interrogator at last took notice of me. "What's wrong, Wladimir Martinovich? Why are you not signing the pages as you read them?" At last I was forced to answer, so I said, far too weakly: "I can't sign this the way it's written. It's not what I said or did. You know I'm not the spy you describe so cleverly and completely in this report."

At these words, my gentle and friendly interrogator changed completely. He grew pale and furious, unable to speak at first, trembling with the intensity of his anger. Only after several deep breaths could he force himself to say, quietly and icily: "Do you realize, you stupid American, the seriousness of this final procedure? It's a matter of life and death you are fooling around with. Do you understand? Either you sign the document as it is, without any change, or we will get rid of you the same way we get rid of every spy. There is a bloody war going on outside. If you don't sign those pages, I can sign one right here and you'll be dead before the sun sets! This is the end, one way or another. Do what you're supposed to do, or die!" I was literally stunned into submission. The sudden, vehement change in the interrogator, the quaver in his voice that lent a note of terror and urgency to his threats, my own interior turmoil and confusion, the shock of it all. Spontaneously, without thinking, I picked up the pen and began to sign.

As I signed the pages, largely without reading them, I began to burn with shame and guilt. I was totally broken, totally humiliated. It was a moment of agony I'll never forget as long as I live. I was full of fear and yet tormented by conscience. After signing the first hundred pages, I stopped even the pretense of reading the rest. I just wanted to finish signing them as quickly as possible and get out of the interrogator's office. My aversion to the whole thing was overwhelming; I condemned myself before anybody else could do the same. I was despicable in my own eyes, no less than I must appear to others. My will had failed; I had proved to be nowhere near the man I thought I was. I had yielded, in that one sickening split second, to fear, to threats, to the thought of death. When the last page was finished, I literally wanted to run from the interrogator's office.

Back in my cell, I stood shaken and defeated. At first, I could not even grasp the dimensions of what had happened to me in the interrogator's office and why. I was tormented by feelings of defeat, failure, and guilt. Yet above all, I was burning with shame. Physically, I shook with spasms of nervous tension and release. When at last I began to regain some control of my nerves, my thoughts, and my emotions, I turned at once to prayer as best I could.

My prayer at first, though, was a matter of reproaches. I reproached myself for failing to stand up against the interrogator and speak out, for failing to refuse to sign the dossier. I reproached myself for caving in out of fear, for giving way to panic, and acting sheerly out of some defense mechanism. And I did not spare God from these reproaches. Why had he failed me at the critical juncture? Why had he not sustained my strength and my nerve? Why had he not inspired me to speak out boldly? Why had he not shielded me by his grace from the fear of death? And why had he not, as a last resort, seen to it that I suffered a heart attack from all this tension, or a stroke, so that I would not have been able to sign the papers? I had trusted in him and his Spirit to give me a voice and wisdom against all adversaries. I had confounded no one, but had myself been totally broken and confounded. And if I was not worth his intervention personally, how could he have allowed me to sign things that reflected so badly upon the Church? Were not his honor and his glory and the future of his kingdom upon earth at stake in all of this?

Little by little, surely under his inspiration and his grace, I began to wonder about myself and my prayer. Why did I feel this way? The sense of defeat and failure was easy enough to explain after that episode in the interrogator's office, but why so strong a sense of guilt and shame? I had acted in panic, I had yielded under the threat of death. Why should I hold myself so fully responsible, why feel so guilty, for actions taken without full deliberation or full consent of the will? I had not been fully responsible at that moment, I had been nearly out of my mind. The act of signing had been prompted by an almost animal-like urge for survival. It had hardly been conscious and surely not deliberate enough to deserve the name human. I had failed, true; but how much guilt had there been and why should I feel so ashamed?

Slowly, reluctantly, under the gentle proddings of grace, I faced the truth that was at the root of my problem and my shame. The answer was a single word: I. I was ashamed because I knew in my heart that I had tried to do too much on my own, and I had failed. I felt guilty because I realized, finally, that I had asked for God's help but had really believed in my own ability to avoid evil and to meet every challenge. I had spent much time in prayer over the years, I had come to appreciate and thank God for his providence and care of me and of all men, but I had never really abandoned myself to it. In a way, I had been thanking God all the while that I was not like the rest of men, that he had given me a good physique, steady nerves, and a strong will, and that with these physical graces given by God I would continue to do his will at all times and to the best of *my* ability. In short, I felt guilty and ashamed because in the last analysis I had relied almost completely on myself in this most critical test—and I had failed.

Had I not even set the terms upon which the Holy Spirit was to intervene in my behalf? Had I not expected him to prompt me to give an answer I had already predetermined was the answer I would give? When I failed to feel his promptings along the lines I expected—indeed, that I demanded—I was frustrated and disappointed. It was then I felt he had abandoned me, and I proceeded to try to do on my own what I had already determined was the thing that must be done. I had not really left myself open to the Spirit. I had, in fact, long ago decided what I expected to hear from the Spirit and when I did not hear precisely *that* I had felt betrayed. Whatever else the Spirit might have been telling me at that hour, I could not hear. I was so intent on hearing only one message, the message I wanted to hear, that I was not really listening at all.

This tendency to set acceptable conditions upon God, to seek unconsciously to make his will for us coincide with our desires, is a very human trait. And the more important the situation is, the more totally we are committed to it or the more completely our future depends upon it, then the easier it becomes for us to blind ourselves into thinking that what we want is surely what God must also want. We can see but one solution only, and naturally we assume that God will help us reach it. In any case, I am sure that this tendency was strong in me. I had been strong-willed as a boy. When I entered religion, I saw this character trait as a talent given me by God rather than as a flaw. I took pride in developing it further, through ascetical practices such as fasting, severe penances, exercises of will, and personal discipline. Had I failed to see that these were not always done solely in response to God's grace or out of some apostolic motive, but also out of pride? Yes, I prided myself on doing these things better or more often than others, vying as it were with the legends of the saints to prove that *I* (that telltale word, again) could prove their equal and somehow be better than my contemporaries.

It is an awful thing, this dross of self that spoils even the best things we do out of the supposedly highest motives. "Like gold in the furnace He tried them," says the Book of Wisdom about the souls of the just. Somehow, by the trials and tribulations of this life, our souls must be purified of this dross of self if we are to become ultimately acceptable to God. For each of us the trials will come in different ways and at different times—for some, self may be easier to overcome than for others—but we were created to do God's will and not our own, to make our own wills conform to his and not vice versa. We can daily pray for the grace to do this, without always meaning it; we can promise quite easily in prayer that we will do it. What we fail to see is how much of self still resides in that promise, how much we are trusting in our own powers when we say that *we* will do it. In large tests or small, therefore, God must sometimes allow us to act on our own so we can learn humility, so we can learn the truth of our total dependence on him, so we can learn that all our actions are sustained by his grace and that without him we can do nothing—not even make our own mistakes.

Learning the full truth of our dependence upon God and our relation to his will is what the virtue of humility is all about. For humility is truth, the full truth, the truth that encompasses our relation to God the Creator and through him to the world he has created and to our fellowmen. And what we call humiliations are the trials by which our more complete grasp of this truth is tested. It is self that is humiliated; there would be no "humiliation" if we had learned to put self in its place, to see ourselves in proper perspective before God and other men. And the stronger the ingredient of self develops in our lives, the more severe must our humiliations be in order to purify us. That was the terrible insight that dawned upon me in the cell at Lubianka as I prayed, shaken and dejected, after my experience with the interrogator.

The Spirit had not abandoned me, for the whole experience had been his work. The sense of guilt and shame I felt was rooted in my failure to put grace ahead of nature, my failure to trust primarily in God rather than in my own powers. I had failed and I was shaken to the roots, but it was a salutary shaking. If the interrogator's threat had been totally sincere, then the moment had been a matter of life and death. In that moment, I had not seen death as God sees it or as I professed to believe it. Just as I had always seen the sessions with the interrogator from beginning to end, sometimes consciously, often unconsciously, as a contest between his will and my own, so in this moment of total crisis I had seen death almost solely in terms of self and not as the moment of my return to God, as it truly is. I had reason, therefore, to feel shame and guilt. It had been a moment of utter failure on my part to abandon myself to God's will in total Christian commitment; I had failed miserably to be what I professed to be, or to act according to the principles I professed to believe. And yet that moment of failure was in itself a great grace, for it had taught me a great lesson. Severe as the test had been, God had sustained me and was now instructing me by the light of his grace.

"He who endures to the end will be saved." That is the conclusion of all the Gospel texts which speak of trusting the Spirit and worrying not in advance what we shall say in times of persecution. I had taken those texts literally and expected the Spirit to instruct me so that I might conquer my interrogator, my persecutor. How foolish and how selfish! It was not the Church that was on trial in Lubianka. It was not the Soviet Government or the NKVD versus Walter Ciszek. It was God versus Walter Ciszek. God was testing me by this experience, like gold in the furnace, to see how much of self remained after all my prayers and professions of faith in his will. In that one year of interrogations, these last terrible few hours, the primacy of self that had manifested itself and been reinforcing itself even in my methods of prayer and spiritual exercises underwent a purging, through purgatory, that left me cleansed to the bone. It was a pretty hot furnace, to say the least, very nearly as hot as hell itself. Yet, thanks be to God, I did still endure—and I had learned, to the depths of my shaken soul, how totally I depended on him for everything even in my survival and how foolish had been my reliance upon self.

Somehow, that day, I imagined I must know how Saint Peter felt when he had survived his denials and been restored to Christ's friendship. Even though our Lord had promised that he, being once converted, would confirm his brethren, I doubt very much that Peter ever again boasted that he would never desert the Lord even if all others deserted him. I find it perfectly understandable that Peter, in his letters to the early churches, should have reminded his Christians to work out their salvation in fear and trembling. For just as surely as man begins to trust in his own abilities, so surely has he taken the first step on the road to ultimate failure. And the greatest grace God can give such a man is to send him a trial he cannot bear with his own powers—and then sustain him with his grace so he may endure to the end and be saved.

Chapter Seven

FOUR YEARS OF PURGATORY

Two weeks after I signed the false dossier admitting to things I had never done, I was informed of the punishment for my "crimes". Fifteen years at hard labor. The verdict was in the form of what was called an administrative sentence, not a judicial verdict. Since I had never been brought to trial of any sort, it was not passed by a court or a panel of judges. The verdict was simply assigned on my own admission of guilt. No matter the niceties, fifteen years was fifteen years.

At least, I thought, the torture of interrogations is over. I even looked forward to Siberia and hard labor: physical suffering had merely to be endured; it entailed no shame or guilt. My prayer at this period was no longer of petition and surely not of consolation. It was a prayer of suffering, of doubts, of fears, and of anxieties. I was so shaken by the revelation and realization of my own weakness that I doubted my ability to survive another onslaught on my faith. I was afraid I would, somehow, sometime, lose sight of God and fail completely. I longed for the day when I would leave this prison and set out for the labor camps. It would be a fresh start, a new life. Then perhaps I could forget my mistakes and my weaknesses, and begin again a more faithful service of God.

But it was not to be. There were to be four more years of interrogations and testing in Lubianka before the Lord was finished tempering and purifying my soul. It was not enough for me to understand that the experience of Lubianka was designed by God to purge me of dependence upon self and to lead me to reliance only upon him. After the terrible time of the past year and its ultimate crisis, I had come at last to understand that truth.

But understanding of itself does not lead to practice or accomplishment; and it was to the practice of purgation that I was now led.
I was told by the interrogator at first that this was a period of "clarification". There were things that had to be cleared up, things we had not as yet gone into sufficiently. Since I had now agreed to cooperate, since I in fact had cooperated by signing the dossier, he was sure that these next sessions would be most productive. For my part, I felt an immediate surge of repugnance and foreboding. I was tremendously afraid. Having failed once, I was literally terrified that I might fail completely this time and lose the last thing I still clung to, my faith in God. And I felt trapped. The mistake I had made in signing was now being used as a lever to force me further. I cursed myself again for having made such a mistake, but I could find no way back. The future seemed hopelessly marked by that one moment of failure.

I was so desolate that even prayer seemed impossible. I felt endangered and threatened anew, but I could find no light or consolation in prayer. I found myself instead reproaching God for not sparing me this new ordeal. I found myself wondering why he permitted it to go on, day after day, without finding some way to end it, or helping me to find a way to step back from the downward path I seemed to be moving along.

For "cooperation", it now appeared, involved something more than just clearing up some things discussed in earlier sessions. Cooperation now came to mean that I should actively work with them in any number of schemes that were suggested one after the other. Life in the camp was painted in its blackest and bitterest details, and it was pointed out to me how easily I could escape all that if I wanted to work for the NKVD. I was annoyed, and then ashamed again of my own indecisiveness. Why couldn't I just stand up and say no? Instead, I temporized. I took to playing a game of cat and mouse with the interrogator, asking for time to think over his various proposals.

He never seemed to have any doubt that I would ultimately cooperate. He arranged to have books provided for me, so I could spend my time in reading. They were largely books on the history or philosophy of communism, or the writings of Marx or Lenin.

When we got together afterwards, the interrogator would quiz me to see if I understood the arguments and how I felt about them. I began to rely again on my own native wit and intelligence, to prolong the arguments and thereby to postpone the need for any practical decision to cooperate. And yet I felt sick at heart, because I knew that every step I took along this path would make it just that much more difficult and dangerous to refuse in the end to cooperate. Lie once and innocence is lost forever. Fall once, and the vessel is broken. Perhaps it can be mended and made serviceable again, but it can never again be as good as new. So it is with fallen human nature or the broken human spirit. Tortured by such thoughts, I grew increasingly depressed.

On the other hand, the interrogator grew bolder and more confident. He was so sure I was moving to join him that he even suggested a young girl for me to marry. I managed to convince him that my whole training up to this point as a priest ill suited me for marriage, and that it was hardly fair to the girl. He seemed to see the logic of this, and I won that argument. Then he suggested that, since I wanted to remain a priest, I should become a member of the Orthodox Church. He explained how easy it would be for him to arrange that, and also to arrange for me to have a platform from which I might denounce the Pope. He stressed how the Orthodox Church, unlike the Catholic Church, has condemned fascism and was helping the government in the war against totalitarianism. But the Popes had attacked communism, especially Pius XII, who surely must secretly sympathize with Mussolini and Hitler. That led to long arguments about the Church. Finally, I managed to convince him that the Catholic Church was, to me, at least as meaningful as the Communist Party was to him. I felt toward her the same sense of loyalty and allegiance that he felt to the Communist Party. I could not help it; it was part of me. So we agreed to disagree, and I felt I had won another round.

All this time, I was growing more and more depressed. Whatever little victories I might be winning, I knew that I was simply postponing the inevitable. I asked in prayer for courage and wisdom to face each new argument, yet deep down I knew that it was all a big mistake. Every time I brought myself to the brink of calling a halt to the proceedings, though, of taking some firm stand, I faced again that awful moment of decision and of weakness—and finally of indecision. I could not do it. And I knew that every time I approached that decision and failed to make it, the harder it would ultimately be to make.

Then one day the blackness closed in around me completely. Perhaps it was brought on by exhaustion, but I reached a point of despair. I was overwhelmed by the hopelessness of my situation. I knew that I was approaching the end of my ability to postpone a decision. I could see no way out of it. Yes, I despaired in the most literal sense of the word: I lost all sense of hope. I saw only my own weakness and helplessness to choose either position open to me, cooperation or execution. There had been no mention recently of the prison camps; the interrogator had been telling me he must make a progress report to his superior about my cooperation; he spoke of execution as if it was possible at their whim. It wasn't the thought of death that bothered me. In fact, I sometimes thought of death by suicide as the only way out of this dilemma. Illogical, surely, but despondency and despair are like that. Uppermost in my mind was the hopelessness of it all and my powerlessness to cope with it.

I don't really know how to put that moment in words. I'm not sure, even, how long that moment lasted. But I know that when it passed I was horrified and bewildered; I knew that I had gone beyond all bounds, had crossed over the brink into a fit of blackness I had never known before. It was very real and I began to tremble. I was scared and ashamed, the victim of a new sense of guilt and humiliation. I had been afraid before, but now I was afraid of myself. I knew I had failed before, but this was the ultimate failure. This was despair. For that one moment of blackness, I had lost not only hope but the last shreds of my faith in God. I had stood alone in a void and I had not even thought of or recalled the one thing that had been my constant guide, my only source of consolation in all other failures, my ultimate recourse: I had lost the sight of God.

Recognizing that, I turned immediately to prayer in fear and trembling. I knew I had to seek immediately the God I had forgotten. I had to ask that that moment of despair had not made me unworthy of his help. I had to pray that he would never again let me fail to remember him and trust in him. I pleaded my helplessness to face the future without him. I told him that my own abilities were now bankrupt and he was my only hope. Suddenly, I was consoled by thoughts of our Lord and his agony in the garden. "Father," he had said, "if it be possible, let this chalice pass from me." In the Garden of Olives, he too knew the feeling of fear and weakness in his human nature as he faced suffering and death. Not once but three times did he ask to have his ordeal removed or somehow modified. Yet each time he concluded with an act of total abandonment and submission to the Father's will. "Not as I will, but as thou wilt." It was not just conformity to the will of God; it was total self-surrender, a stripping away of all human fears, of all doubts about his own abilities to withstand the passion, of every last shred of self including self-doubt.

What a wonderful treasure and source of strength and consolation our Lord's agony in the garden became for me from that moment on. I saw clearly exactly what I must do. I can only call it a conversion experience, and I can only tell you frankly that my life was changed from that moment on. If my moment of despair had been a moment of total blackness, then this was an experience of blinding light. I knew immediately what I must do, what I would do, and somehow I knew that I could do it. I knew that I must abandon myself entirely to the will of the Father and live from now on in this spirit of self-abandonment to God. And I did it. I can only describe the experience as a sense of "letting go", giving over totally my last effort or even any will to guide the reins of my own life. It is all too simply said, yet that one decision has affected every subsequent moment of my life. I have to call it a conversion.

I had always trusted in God. I had always tried to find his will, to see his providence at work. I had always seen my life and my destiny as guided by his will. At some moments more consciously than at others, I had been aware of his promptings, his call, his promises, his grace. At times of crisis, especially, I had tried to discover his will and to follow it to the best of my ability. But this was a new vision, a totally new understanding, something more than just a matter of emphasis. Up until now, I had always seen my role—man's role—in the divine economy as an active one. Up to this time, I had retained in my own hands the reins of all decision, actions, and endeavors; I saw it now as my task to "cooperate" with his grace, to be involved to the end in the working out of salvation. God's will was "out there" somewhere, hidden, yet clear and unmistakable. It was my role—man's role—to discover what it was and then conform my will to that, and so work at achieving the ends of his divine providence. I remained—man remained—in essence the master of my own destiny. Perfection consisted simply in learning to discover God's will in every situation and then in bending every effort to do what must be done.

Now, with sudden and almost blinding clarity and simplicity, I realized I had been trying to do something with my own will and intellect that was at once too much and mostly all wrong. God's will was not hidden somewhere "out there" in the situations in which I found myself; the situations themselves *were* his will for me. What he wanted was for me to accept these situations as from his hands, to let go of the reins and place myself entirely at his disposal. He was asking of me an act of total trust, allowing for no interference or restless striving on my part, no reservations, no exceptions, no areas where I could set conditions or seem to hesitate. He was asking a complete gift of self, nothing held back. It demanded absolute faith: faith in God's existence, in his providence, in his concern for the minutest detail, in his power to sustain me, and in his love protecting me. It meant losing the last hidden doubt, the ultimate fear that God will not be there to bear you up. It was something like that awful eternity between anxiety and belief when a child first leans back and lets go of all support whatever—only to find that the water truly holds him up and he can float motionless and totally relaxed.

Once understood, it seemed so simple. I was amazed it had taken me so long in terms of time and of suffering to learn this truth. Of course we believe that we depend on God, that his will sustains us in every moment of our life. But we are afraid to put it to the test. There remains deep down in each of us a little nagging doubt, a little knot of fear which we refuse to face or admit even to ourselves, that says, "Suppose it isn't so." We are afraid to abandon ourselves totally into God's hands for fear he will not catch us as we fall. It is the ultimate criterion, the final test of all faith and all belief, and it is present in each of us, lurking unvoiced in a closet of our mind we are afraid to open. It is not really a question of trust in God at all, for we want very much to trust him; it is really a question of our ultimate belief in his existence and his providence, and it demands the purest act of faith.

For my part, I was brought to make this perfect act of faith, this act of complete self-abandonment to his will, of total trust in his love and concern for me and his desire to sustain and protect me, by the experience of a complete despair of my own powers and abilities that had preceded it. I knew I could no longer trust myself, and it seemed only sensible then to trust totally in God. It was the grace God had been offering me all my life, but which I had never really had the courage to accept in full. I had talked of finding and doing his will, but never in the sense of totally giving up my own will. I had talked of trusting him, indeed I truly had trusted him, but never in the sense of abandoning all other sources of support and relying on his grace alone. I could never find it in me, before, to give up self completely. There were always boundaries beyond which I would not go, little hedges marking out what I knew in the depths of my being was a point of no return. God in his providence had been constant in his grace, always providing opportunities for this act of perfect faith and trust in him, always urging me to let go the reins and trust in him alone. I had trusted him, I had cooperated with his grace—but only up to a point. Only when I had reached a point of total bankruptcy of my own powers had I at last surrendered.

That moment, that experience, completely changed me. I can say it now in all sincerity, without false modesty, without a sense either of exaggeration or of embarrassment. I have to call it a conversion experience; it was at once a death and a resurrection. It was not something I sought after or wanted or worked for or merited. Like every grace, it was a free gift of God. That it should have been offered to me when I had reached the limits of my own powers is simply part of the great mystery of salvation. I did not question it then; I cannot question it now. Nor can I explain how that one experience could have such an immediate and lasting effect upon my soul and upon my habitual actions from that moment on, especially when so many other experiences, so many other graces, had had no such effect. It was, however, a deliberate act of choice on my part. I know it was a choice I never could have made, and never had made before, without the inspiration of God's grace. But it was a deliberate choice. I chose, consciously and willingly, to abandon myself to God's will, to let go completely of every last reservation. I knew I was crossing a boundary I had always hesitated and feared to cross before. Yet this time I chose to cross it—and the result was a feeling not of fear but of liberation, not of danger or of despair but a fresh new wave of confidence and of happiness.

Across that threshold I had been afraid to cross, things suddenly seemed so very simple. There was but a single vision, God, who was all in all; there was but one will that directed all things, God's will. I had only to see it, to discern it in every circumstance in which I found myself, and let myself be ruled by it. God is in all things, sustains all things, directs all things. To discern this in every situation and circumstance, to see his will in all things, was to accept each circumstance and situation and let oneself be borne along in perfect confidence and trust. Nothing could separate me from him, because he was in all things. No danger could threaten me, no fear could shake me, except the fear of losing sight of him. The future, hidden as it was, was hidden in his will and therefore acceptable to me no matter what it might bring. The past, with all its failures, was not forgotten; it remained to remind me of the weakness of human nature and the folly of putting any faith in self. But it no longer depressed me. I looked no longer to self to guide me, relied on it no longer in any way, so it could not again fail me. By renouncing, finally and completely, all control of my life and future destiny, I was relieved as a consequence of all responsibility. I was freed thereby from anxiety and worry, from every tension, and could float serenely upon the tide of God's sustaining providence in perfect peace of soul.

Filled with this new spirit and transformed interiorly, I no longer dreaded the next interview with the interrogator. I saw no reason now to fear him or the NKVD, for I saw all things now as coming from the hands of God. I was no longer afraid of making a "mistake", since God's will was behind every development and every alternative. Secure in his grace, I felt capable of facing every situation and meeting every challenge; whatever he chose to send me in the future, I would accept.

The change in me, in fact, was so striking that even the interrogator noticed it. His newest proposal was that I might serve as chaplain in a newly formed army of Polish communists under Wanda Wasilewski, or perhaps as chaplain in General Ander's army, an army of Free Poles formed to fight on the proposed second front. I told him quite simply I was willing to do either. He seemed genuinely pleased with the promptness of my reply and my new disposition. He told me that I seemed more relaxed and easy in my mind—as indeed I was, because the fear of making a mistake had left me now that I was conscious God was with me. I think he was suspicious, though, of this sudden change of heart. "Good," he said, "I'll tell the people upstairs that you are ready and willing to act as chaplain wherever you're sent. I'll let you know their answer as soon as I hear."

The next time I saw him, however, he had a new proposal. He told me that the people upstairs wanted me, instead, to go to Rome and serve as an intermediary between the Kremlin and the Vatican. Now that the Soviet Union was a member of the Allies, perhaps a sort of concordat about communism could be arranged. I agreed, as far-fetched and absurd as it all sounded. The notion of returning to Rome, to the free world, might in the past have excited me—but it was a measure of my new sense of abandonment that I was not the least excited by this offer more than any other. Whether I went to Rome or not was for God to decide, for him to arrange. I stood ready to accept any and all events as coming from his hand. Discussions of this Roman business took up many sessions with the interrogator, yet through it all I remained totally detached and perfectly relaxed. Naturally, the interrogator explained, I would not be alone in Rome. I would be part of a team and there would be other information I would be asked to pass along, other details I would be expected to provide for transmission back to Moscow. Should I fail to do so, should I betray this trust, those with whom I worked would see to my speedy execution. Before I left for Rome, there would be a month's training in certain techniques of espionage that I would probably need in Rome.

Through all this, I remained at peace. Where before, the notion of such cooperation would have upset and tormented me, I felt no such distress any longer. If these things were to be, then they were to be—for a purpose God alone knew. If they were not to be, then they would never happen. My confidence in his will and his providence was absolute; I knew I had only to follow the promptings of his grace. I was sure, completely sure, that when a moment of decision came he would lead me on the right path. And so it happened. When at last the interrogator asked me to sign an agreement covering the Roman business, I just refused. I had not thought of doing so in advance; in fact, I had simply gone along with everything up to that point. But suddenly it seemed the only thing to do, and I did it. He became violently angry and threatened me with immediate execution. I felt no fear at all. I think I smiled. I knew then I had won. When he called for the guards to lead me away—and I had no assurance but that they were leading me before a firing squad—I went with them as if they were so many ministers of grace. I felt his presence in the moment and knew it drew me toward a future of his design and purpose. I wished for nothing more.

Chapter Eight

IN TRANSIT

I left Lubianka, as it turned out, not to face a firing squad but to begin the long journey from Moscow to Siberia, and I was overjoyed. Packed into the prison trains like so many head of cattle during the grinding, seemingly endless trip, or herded into already overcrowded and primitive transfer camps and stockades, we were subjected to conditions that were deplorable—even subhuman— and yet I was delighted simply to be with people once again. To my surprise, eager as I was for companionship and conversation, I found it difficult at first to talk to others. I listened curiously and avidly while they talked, but spoke little myself. My mind seemed to be on some other track; it was hard for me sometimes even to grasp what they were talking about. It was a strange sort of disorientation, brought on I suppose from the long periods in solitary confinement and the defensive mental habits developed during the sessions of interrogation. I found it a real strain, at first, trying to converse with the other prisoners. Still, just being with others and hearing them talk was enough to buoy me up. I did not know for sure what lay at the end of this journey, or specifically where I was going, but for the moment that was of little consequence. I was still a prisoner, but I felt free and liberated. It was almost as if I had risen from the tomb of Lubianka.

I found myself quite literally hungering for news of what had happened during my five years of imprisonment, to say nothing of current news. I did know that the war in Europe had ended during my last year in Lubianka. The bells in nearby Red Square had pealed excitedly, and the news caused so much excitement and joy that one of the guards happily spread the word to the prisoners. It was one of the few times I learned anything about the outside world during those years. So now I craved information about the war, about the regime, about other prisoners, about the world at large. I was curious beyond belief, almost addicted to stories of every sort, even rumors. The habit of recollection I had been able to develop while in solitary confinement broke down under this bombardment. I was continuously distracted, even when I tried to pray. The quiet, interior contacts with God I had enjoyed in prison, periods of reflection or of contemplation, were less effective and frequent now.

Nor was that the only adjustment I had to make. My desire to see God's will in every situation, to search out and understand his providence at work in every circumstance, now began to bump up against the real world once more. It had been easy during the periods of prayer and contemplation to imagine future happenings and the way I would try to respond to them. In the light of the vision I then enjoyed, it was easy to float freely and euphorically into the future, ready to accept whatever God might have prepared for me there. But the future was now the present and, as is always the case, it was a lot more unmanageable and full of bustle than it had seemed in the abstract. Accordingly, my new spirit of interior resolve to search out and understand and accept God's will in every detail of every situation was quickly put to a rude test by the rough and ready realities of life. To put it another way, I had been alone with God as it were on the mountaintop, but now I had to come down once more into the hubbub, turmoil, and dissension of the camp.

And, somewhat like Moses, the first thing I discovered was the presence of evil. Not as an abstract idea or philosophical definition, but as an ugly reality, brutal, harsh, uncompromisingly cruel. For most of my journey across the vast stretches of the Russian Steppes, in the crude confines of the prison trains or the primitive transit camps, I traveled to Siberia with hardcase criminals. Not political prisoners like myself, but the thugs who people the Russian underworld—or for that matter, I guess, any underworld. They were hard and tough and mean, with their own set of principles, their own standards of behavior, their own set of values. Force and deception were the virtues they admired; if conscience meant anything at all, it was simply as a sign of weakness. They had long since learned to despise it and to live by their own code. They were absolutely ruthless and without scruple. Accordingly, they rode roughshod over the political prisoners with whom they came in contact; even the armed guards were afraid to interfere with them much or antagonize them.

They did not hesitate to kill on the slightest provocation. Physical violence for them was simply the way to acquire mastery over and inspire fear in others. Among themselves, there was a certain hierarchy based on strength and toughness and mindless cruelty. But they were united against all "others"; they stuck together, they shared an attitude of despising anyone who was not one of them. They seemed particularly to resent and pick upon the political prisoners. They would call them traitors, and felt thereby somehow justified in looking down on them. And because the politicals were largely educated men, or former party men, they castigated them as "tools of the NKVD". All this, in their own code, gave them some sort of right to dominate and brutalize the political prisoners. They took from them, as a matter of course and without question, whatever they wanted in the way of food or clothing. Any attempt at resistance or opposition was met by physical violence. Might made right. Beatings were administered without mercy or compunction.

The criminal world, the criminal mind, was something entirely new to me. It was at once horrifying and yet fascinating. For the first time I palpably experienced the power of evil and how completely it could overshadow the power of good. Good men, under the circumstances, were simply no match for those who would lie, steal, bully, beat, curse, or even kill without scruple. A man would have to give up everything that was best in him, descend to the level of animal instinct and passion and hate, in order to compete with these men or respond in kind. And even then he would be no match for them in raw physical violence or brutality. For these men were held back by nothing, they felt no restraint, they had grown accustomed to a jungle where the strongest and most savage ruled and the weaker managed to survive by unprincipled cunning. And what they did, they did openly. They were secure and unchallenged in the world they inhabited, a world with its own codes and rules and values as absolute as any "code of morality" ever devised. Yet totally perverted.

What was more, they simply took for granted their domination of other prisoners, as if they were destined from all eternity to rule over the universe of the prisons and prison camps by some divine right. It was the arrogance of evil that made it so frightening. There was no avenue of recourse, except to become as evil and perverted yourself and retaliate in kind. Some political prisoners did resort to this when their numbers permitted. But the underworld's domination of this prison universe is rooted in terror, and it has both a long memory and an organizational code that makes it possible to retaliate with terror at another time and in some other place. Later in the camps, for example, I saw thugs walk into a barracks, pull from his bunk a political prisoner who, with his friends, had beaten up a criminal who was bullying them earlier in another camp, and stomp him to death while the rest of the men in the barracks stood stunned and silent. The underworld boasted of its ability to revenge its own, and it was because of the fear such threats of retaliation engendered that its reign went largely unchallenged.

I had seen some of this in the prison at Perm. I had experienced hardly any of it for the last five years in Lubianka, because of the solitary nature of confinement there and because the vast majority of those confined at Lubianka were political prisoners. But now I was rudely reintroduced to it. On the prison train that took me out of Moscow, I was confined in a compartment with twenty thieves and criminals. I was the only political prisoner among them. As soon as I was shoved into the compartment by the guards, I was completely at their mercy. They took my extra clothes, which they then bartered with the guards for more food—for themselves alone. They openly dared me to make a remark or do anything about it. When I glared at the leader of the group in silent anger, he cursed me, told me he didn't like the way I was looking at him, and threatened to have his companions beat me into submission.

It was a rough reintroduction to the real world. I experienced physical fear, interior anger, and a certain amount of spiritual confusion. This was the situation, these were the people, I kept trying to tell myself, that formed the will of God for me today. I was not amused by these rather rueful reflections, but I was confused. Unable for the moment even to pray or recollect myself, I sat in a corner of the prison-car compartment and watched anxiously what went on about me.

I thought about the necessities of life. It suddenly occurred to me how little I had ever had to worry about such things in the past. Even in prison, such things as food, shelter, and clothing— poor as they might have been—had been provided for me. In a sense, in the words of the Gospel, I had not had to worry what I was going to eat or drink or wear or where I would sleep—all this had been given to me in some fashion during my religious life or in the work camps or prisons of the Soviet Union—I had only to worry about the kingdom of God and his justice! Now, as I watched the thieves and criminals providing for themselves in a universe with its own set of standards and "justice", I began to wonder about my own survival. The children of this world, surely, were wiser than the children of light. How would I survive among them? For them, nothing existed beyond this material world and this moment. They survived because they had learned how to survive. They were masters of the art of survival. Outside the bounds of civilized behavior or conscience, they preyed upon anyone weaker than themselves and revenged them- selves upon society by crimes of violence and theft. In their view, society owed them something. So they took it. It was as simple as that.

In all this, I could not help but think how different their outlook on life and their beliefs were from my own. It was not a thought that sprang out of any notion of how much better I was, how superior I was to them. Just the opposite, in fact. I felt out of place with them, like an alien or an outcast. I was shocked by their language, with its routine use of blasphemy, but that was nothing compared to the gulf between their whole view of life and mine. We had almost nothing in common, except perhaps our human instinct for survival, an instinct that was causing me at the moment to tremble a little. For the rest, they scorned every value I esteemed. What I considered virtues, for them were simply signs of weakness; in their code of morality, everything I had considered a sin was looked upon as a virtue. They were atheists, materialists, opportunists, and absolutely unscrupulous.

As I lived with men like these during the long years in the prison camps, I slowly learned that such initial impressions were not altogether accurate. Little by little, I came to understand that underneath their violent exterior and twisted moral code these criminals were men, too; men driven by fear, perhaps more so than most men, but still men nonetheless. Like all men they had had their share of hopes once; like all men they could be haunted still by memories—of family, of loved ones, of better times now lost, of opportunities missed. In a sense, they were men banded together in a world of their own out of the same basic drive for friendship and for comradeship (even if in crime) that all men feel, out of the same need for a sense of belonging and of security, out of the same need to share a common goal and set of values— though for them this often meant revenge upon society. Understanding all this in later years never led me to accept or condone their actions in any way, but I did learn to pity them as human beings even as I feared them for what they were and what they might do. For the moment, however, in this prison car, all I knew was the fear; all I could see now was the worst side of these men, and I sat thinking apprehensively of my future among them

What would the men I would meet in the prison camps toward which I was heading be like? Would they be like these professional criminals? Would they have adopted the values and the attitudes of these prisoners in order to get along in the world of the prison camps and to survive? If so, where would I fit in? Would I, too, have to adopt the wisdom of the children of this world in order to get enough food and clothing to survive in the world of the slave labor camps? Would I be able to take care of myself?

I realized almost immediately that I was asking the questions, raising the doubts, that I had promised not to ask in abandoning myself to the will of God. And I realized, too, that it's one thing to give up such doubts and questions in a moment of grace and inspiration and spiritual insight, but another thing to prevent them from arising spontaneously when the harsh and rough circumstances of a moment of daily life drives from the mind everything except thoughts of here and now. So I did not feel ashamed of such doubts and questions; I simply recognized them for what they were and tried to recollect myself to recapture my commitment to God's will even under these circumstances.

I did not know how I would react in the world into which I had been so rudely thrust and in which my future life would be lived for as far forward as I could see. I only knew that it would be my life and that it was the life God wanted me to live. I was to be a laborer in a vineyard in which the laborers might be very few indeed. The harvest, however, would not depend on me but upon God's providence, even as had the sowing of the seed. I did not really know what God might expect of me in all details, nor did I know how much I could expect of myself. But that was precisely why I had resolved to accept all things, come what may, as from his hands.

I thought again of that text: "The children of this world are wiser than the children of light." It seemed a peculiar thing to keep running through my mind, and yet a strange and exciting challenge for a priest-apostle on a prison train heading for the labor camps. The challenge seemed plain. Could my sacrifice, could my total dedication, could my stamina in doing the will of God be less than that of the children of this world? They knew that in order to survive a long sentence a man had to face and conquer one day at a time. Had I not resolved to see each day, one day at a time, as a gift of God within whose confines I was to accomplish his will? The prisoners survived by taking life as it came, rolling with the punches, hoping only to survive each day as it happened, one day at a time. Surely my motivation ought to help me see beyond that. Each day to me should be more than an obstacle to be gotten over, a span of time to be endured, a sequence of hours to be survived. For me, each day came forth from the hand of God newly created and alive with opportunities to do his will. For me, each day was a series of moments and incidents to be offered back to God, to be consecrated and returned in total dedication to his will. That was what my priesthood demanded of me, as it demanded of every Christian.

The children of this world were dedicated to surviving this life by whatever method possible. I, too, must be totally dedicated, but with an added dimension. I must not seek to avoid hardships or to soften their impact. I must see in them the will of God and through them work out my salvation. Otherwise, I would be acting rather as a child of this world than a child of light. I would be acting not out of faith but as a fatalist. I would have survived a series of moments, a succession of days, but I would have made nothing of them nor of myself. I resolved again, therefore, to accept each day and every moment as from God's hands, and to offer it back to him as best I could. I would not merely passively survive, like the children of this world, but with his help and his grace I would actively participate—and I would survive. I never doubted that, because I did not fear non-survival. Death would simply be a call to return to the God I served each day. My life was to do the will of God, as the prayer our Savior taught us put it quite simply, "On earth as in heaven." His will would determine how long I would spend on earth.

In such thoughts and prayers, peace returned. It was the peace, once again, that total abandonment to God's will brings. Only this time I was not in the quiet confines of a solitary cell in Lubianka, I was in the corner of a rough, jolting, profane prison car. My situation had not improved, but my disposition in the acceptance of God's will had returned. Along with it had come peace and a renewed confidence—not in my own ability to survive, but a total trust and confidence in God's ability to sustain me and provide me with whatever strength I needed to meet the challenges he would send me. What greater peace and confidence could I require? I even looked forward to laboring again in his vineyard.

Chapter Nine

THE BODY

"The spirit indeed is willing but the flesh is weak." How often during the long years in the labor camps did I think of that Scripture text, sometimes in a spirit of gentle irony but mostly in the agony of piercing bodily pain or the despair of total exhaustion. And how often during those years did I think of how much the body means to man, how essential its well-being is to his well-being, how prominent a part in every activity of human existence is played by that clay into which God first breathed the breath of life. "Man is a creature composed of body and soul." We have recited that truth from the day we first learned our catechism. But until the body fails us, or pains us, or forces itself upon our attention by some little twinge or complete collapse, we tend to take for granted this first and most precious of God's gifts to man or to give it short shrift.

My second day in the labor camps was one of those days. The first day was bad enough. I had been put to work shoveling coal in the hold of a ship. The pace was furious. All during the long winter months when the waters were frozen, coal was stored on the banks of the Yenisei River at the arctic port of Dudinka. During the relatively short time each year when the ice melted and the river was navigable, all that coal had to be loaded on ships and moved out. So the prisoners at the Dudinka Camps were driven without rest, twelve to fifteen hours a day in the long arctic summer daylight. It was brutal work to begin with, but I had done no work at all for more than five years. I was physically in no condition to work. But I was marched down to the hold of the ship, given a shovel, and told to spread the coal as it came cascading down a conveyor belt, so that it would be loaded evenly.

I worked until I was ready to drop—which was rather soon because of my condition—and then had to go on working for fear of my life. There was no way I could stop the conveyor belt, and if I stopped shoveling, I would have been buried by the roaring coal. So I had to keep moving, stumbling and slipping over the shifting coal as the hold filled up, working the shovel as best I could even after my arms and chest grew numb and I had no sensation at all in the mechanical motions I made. When I collapsed on the plank bunk of the prison camp that night, every muscle and sinew in my arms and legs, my chest and back, felt completely unstrung.

The morning of the second day, when the signal to rise rang out at 5 A.M., every muscle in my body had stiffened like twisted wrought iron. It was agony even to attempt to get up. The tiniest movement was like a scream of pain. Swinging my legs over the side of the bunk was torture; standing up was a near impossibility. How would I ever march down to the ship, let alone shovel coal for another fifteen hours straight? It couldn't be done. It was physically impossible. But I did it.

That was my introduction to the Siberian labor camps. There was no gradual breaking-in period. After almost five years of constant inactivity in prison, we arrived in the camp one afternoon and began a full day's work the next morning. From then on, unless totally incapacitated by illness or relieved by some other miracle, we worked with hardly a day off. It was the reason we had been sent to these particular camps in the far north. At the transfer camps along the route from Moscow, the sick and the fragile had been screened out. There were no humanitarian motives behind such medical exams, but a policy rather of the sheerest expediency. Siberia, the government had decreed, was to be industrialized; work in that frozen country was a nightmare; despite grand government promises and big bonuses, there were few volunteers; manpower had to be supplied and the prisoners provided it. It was not worthwhile, though, to transport and feed a prisoner unless he could work. If detention were the only purpose to be served, there were plenty of prisons where the sick and the weak and the exhausted could be detained. So those who were sent to the frozen wastes of Siberia were expected to work. And work we did.

Living conditions in the camps were intolerable. The barracks provided just enough shelter from the piercing winds to make survival possible, nothing more. The food ration was just barely enough to sustain life and provide the energy needed to work. There was a "guarantee ration", which was enough to keep you alive; but as an added incentive, there were "plus one", "plus two", and "plus three" coupons for extra rations of food given to those who overfulfilled their quota of work each day. That incentive plan, deliberately or not, could work in reverse upon the prisoners physically. If you failed for several days to fulfill your quota, for example, and were given only the guarantee rations, the weaker you became and the harder it was to fulfill your quota the next day. It was a vicious circle. Yet men survived.

That we survived, under the circumstances, is a tribute to the stubbornness and power of the human will driving the body beyond what a man thought he could endure, and a tribute as well to the marvelous work of God's creation that is the human body. No machine ever devised by man could have withstood, day in and day out, the constant, punishing grind of work in the severest kind of weather that the human body proved itself able to withstand in the Siberian slave labor camps. It is customary to speak of the "indomitable human spirit" as that which carries man through crises like this, but the body surely merits more attention than it usually gets. Not the trained, beautifully conditioned body of the athlete, but the weak, underfed and ordinary body with which we are all endowed. It was under the daily regimen of work to exhaustion in the camps, under the constant torture of hunger and cold, through hurt and pain, distress and disease, weariness beyond comprehension and endurance beyond belief, that I came truly to understand and appreciate the catechism truth that man is a creature composed of body and soul.

There is a strain in Christian asceticism that tends to despise the body, that looks upon it as the corruptible part of man and the source of corruption. Because the soul is immortal and the body is corruptible, Eastern mystics especially tended to look upon the body as a dumb beast that must be beaten into submission like a stubborn ass. "The spirit indeed is willing" to serve God and seek perfection, but "the flesh is weak", is lazy and slothful, is prone to concupiscence and sin, seeks its own pleasures and distracts the soul from seeking God alone. So the early fathers of the Eastern desert, for example, sought to subdue the body by extravagant penances and excessive fasts in order to attain mastery over the weaknesses of the flesh and so free the soul from any tendency to give in to the cravings of this sinful mortal nature. This tendency to look on human nature, especially so-called "fallen human nature", as ignoble and debased, sinful and therefore contemptible, in constant need to be checked and controlled by the nobler part of man, has remained in some form or other a part of traditional Christian spirituality. And I think it is wrong. It is Gnosticism and Manicheism and Catharism and Albigensianism and Jansenism and every heretical tendency that sees matter as evil and the flesh as prone to evil. For whatever reason, it is always the poor old body that gets the worst of it, as if the mind and the will never had any sinful thoughts or inclinations, as if sin did not consist precisely in setting one's will (not the body) against God's will.

What came to me in the prison camps was a tremendous respect and love for the poor old body. It was the body that bore the brunt of all suffering, though the soul might well experience anguish. And it was the body that had to sustain you, for all the strength of will and determination a man might have. It was the body that felt the sting of the wind, the bite of the cold, the cramp of aching muscles, the raw lash of cracked and bleeding flesh, the gnawing agony of hunger in the belly, the soreness and numbness of overtaxed sinews. Frostbite and stomach rumblings, swollen feet, running eyes, chapped lips and battered knuckles, sprains and cramps, and aches and bruises—all these the body patiently endured through the long, long days of labor in the driving snow or freezing rain or spring muck of the Far North, and yet somehow it always managed to get you through one more day. It was the body that underwent the suffering, felt the agony, and carried the heavy weight across its shoulders of this daily passion and slow death of inhuman work. I had always in many ways taken the body for granted. As a youth, I had played at many sports and excelled in some, like baseball and boxing. I had been a scrapper. I had always wanted to outdo everyone, be the best, be the strongest. I could take punishment and I could dish it out. During my early years in religious life, I had even tried to outdo the legends of the saints in fastings and penances of every sort. But I did it not so much to punish the body or attain perfection, as to prove to the world and to myself how tough I was. Yet it was only now, when each day ended with exhaustion and the body cried out for every extra minute of rest, every little respite from work, every extra crumb of food, that I really came to appreciate the marvelous gift of life God had given man in the resources of the human body.

The intimacy that exists between soul and body is a marvel of creation and a mystery of human existence. Yet we do wrong to think, because the soul will be judged after death while the body crumbles in the grave, that this mortal handful of dust is any less a gift of God, any less noble or beautiful than the immortal soul. It is in the body that we exist and work out our salvation. It is in the body that we see and take delight in the beauties of God's created universe, and in the body that we ourselves bear the marks of Christ's passion. The mysterious interplay of body and soul is an essential characteristic of our human nature. If the body is sick or sore, tired or hungry or otherwise distressed, it affects the spirit, affects our judgment, changes our personality. So slight a thing as a headache can affect our relations with those around us. It is through the body that we express and experience love and kindness and comfort. We excuse our snappish, petty, ill-mannered conduct to one another on the grounds that the body is having a bad day. We are constantly, day in and day out, hour after hour, under the influence of these mysterious workings of soul on body and body on soul.

Theologians have written much about the Incarnation as the central act of our redemption, the high point in the drama of salvation history. Spiritual writers can write endlessly about it, talking about redemption and salvific acts, about a new creation and the restructuring of the social order, about mankind being elevated and made once again whole and holy, about expiation and atonement and reconciliation of the fallen world with the divine will, about the new Adam and the kingdom of God and the life of the world to come. What we tend to forget, though, is the very folksy truth that God by his Incarnation took on a human body. We don't often stop to reflect on the most basic meaning of this doctrine: that God, too, knows exactly how it feels to be cold, or tired, or hungry, or sore with pain, because he, too, has had a body. He has spent long hours, for years at a time, doing the routine and unspectacular work of a carpenter, has walked long days over dusty roads with tired feet, has curled his shoulders against the night air or a chill rain, has been without sleep while others slept, has been thirsty and hot and weary and ready to drop from exhaustion.

Christ must have known what it is like to wake up stiff and sore on a dull, gray morning, must have had headaches and toothaches and backaches and aching bones, must have been anxious and annoyed and irritated at times. In the Incarnation God came to know for himself what a thing is the life of man, what a work of his hands is this creature composed of body and soul. From the dark of the womb to the black of the tomb, through childhood to manhood and the last, slow long-drawn-out agony of dying, he has known for himself what it means to live in a handful of clay, to feel the cool touch of mother's hand on fevered flesh, to taste the salt of sweat and tears, to hear music and birdsong and the vilest of insults, to stumble and fall, be bruised and mangled and torn. He cried out at last, as have all of us at one time or another, to be spared any more burdens or suffering. The Incarnation, in short, meant that God became man, like us in all things, says St. Paul, except sin.

Through it all did God find that the body of man was good, as he had pronounced it in the first days of creation? I think so. And through it he achieved our redemption. By redeeming us, he did not thereby free us from our suffering or our pains or our sorrows. Just as his resurrection is our victory and our triumph over death but does not mean we do not have to die, so his passion has redeemed our suffering but does not mean we do not have to suffer or feel pain. Yet his example has taught us how to look upon our suffering in a new way and so to look upon our body in a new light. Redemption, salvation for every individual, consists in doing the will of God, no more and no less; "Father," said Christ at the moment of his supreme agony in the garden, "not my will but thine be done." Yet God will not, has not, asked us to bear any more than he himself has borne in his Incarnation and suffering and death, nor to experience anything he himself did not experience.

For each of us, salvation means no more and no less than taking up daily the same cross of Christ, accepting each day what it brings as the will of God, offering back to God each morning all the joys, works, and sufferings of that day. But those are abstract words. What it means, in practice, is spelled out as always by the poor old body. It means getting up each morning and going to bed exhausted. It means the routine, not the spectacular. It can mean drudgery, pain, putting aside pleasures, happiness, or the love the human heart craves until another time, so that what is necessary at the moment can be done. It means working for others, touching the lives of others, through the medium of the body. How many times, tired and worn out and near collapse from the slave labor conditions of the camps, did I think I could not ask another step of the body, did I think in pain and irony of those words "The spirit indeed is willing but the flesh is weak"? Truly, man is a creature composed of body and soul, and we work out our salvation in this vale of tears through the medium of the flesh. It is the first gift God and our parents fashion for us; it sustains and supports us through a long life and makes possible both joys and sorrows; and when at last we are parted from it in death, it surely deserves whatever rest it can get before it rises to be glorified at the last judgment.

Chapter Ten

WORK

"In the sweat of your brow," God said to Adam in the Garden, "you shall eat your bread till you return to the ground, for out of it you are taken, you are dust, and to dust you shall return." Traditionally, man has looked upon that divine injunction as a curse and upon work as a punishment for sin. Many a man, surely, has looked upon work itself as a curse, a necessary evil—especially the boring, day-to-day labor of a routine job. He does it because by it he earns a living, feeds his family, provides for their welfare and their future and his own security against old age. But he does not have to enjoy it, and by and large he does not. And if ever there was a man for whom work was a curse and a burden without any redeeming features, it must be the worker in a slave labor camp.

For him, Lenin's dictum "who does not work does not eat" is maintained in its severest form. Every labor to which he is driven has been assigned a quota. If he fulfills that quota, he eats. If he does not, he receives just enough rations to keep him alive. And the quota itself is constantly adjusted. If a prisoner fulfills it every day, the quota is soon increased. And if he overfulfills it, in the hope of getting a "plus one" or "plus two" ration, then the amount of work he did in overfulfilling that daily quota becomes his new daily quota. If he wants more food after that, he must overfulfill this new quota. For men driven to work by hunger, and weak enough from starvation, this last turn of the screw is the cruelest game of all.

I had plenty of chance to reflect on the nature of work and the reasons for work during my years in the prison camps of Siberia—

whether it was work on the docks, or in the mines, work out in the unsheltered frozen tundra building a new prison camp from scratch, or work on the construction of new plants to meet the Soviet Government's five-year "industrialization" quotas for the Far North. We worked because we had to work in order to eat, to live, to survive. To work was the purpose of our having been deported to these camps, there was no other reason for our existence. There were millions of us, and it did not really matter to those in charge of the camps who lived and who died; they could not be bothered feeding unproductive mouths. We had been sentenced as enemies of the state; if our work helped to build up the state, it might be considered reparation and we would eventually be freed; if not, then good riddance.

Work was surely a curse under these conditions. The prisoners hated work, they hated the officials who made them work, and they hated the government that had condemned them to these cruel occupations. Only the fact that they had to work to get enough food to live on, to survive, made them report dumbly and mechanically each morning for the labor brigades and march off across the arctic wastes, arms locked behind their backs, to face another day's quota of work. The urge to survive was what made them do it, the thought of survival was all they had to live for and all they lived by. They did as much work as they had to in order to survive, and avoided as much work as they could possibly avoid and still manage to survive. The work was not important, but the food was; and even the food was important only because without it a man could not survive for long. What was important was to get through the day. At the end of each work shift, a man counted the remaining days of his long term and thanked God that one more day had passed.

There was nothing ennobling about work in the slave labor camps. Except for the need to work enough to get enough food to survive, the individual prisoner felt no sense of purpose in the work, experienced no sense of accomplishment. He did not share in the official desire to industrialize the Far North, to set new records of Soviet achievement, to tame the wilderness and tap the wealth of natural resources that lie beneath the frozen Siberian crust. In fact, the men in the labor camps took a certain delight in being able to sabotage the work whenever they could. And even if the brigadiers watched them closely, even if they were forced to fulfill a certain quota of work in order to eat, they still did their best to make sure the work was sloppily done. Far from taking any pride in their work, they found in it a way to revenge themselves on those who had set them to do it.

Not for them the spirit of the Komsomols, or the Young Pioneers, or the Stakhanovites, or the Shock Troops of Communist Labor. Not for them even the simple spirit of the ordinary communist worker, convinced by constant propaganda that hard work is a virtue of "the new Soviet man". Such preaching in the schools, in the newspapers, on radio and TV, in factories and on billboards—makes no distinction between citizens. It demands the self-same sacrifice from the educated and the non-educated, the blue collar worker and the intellectual, the peasant and the city dweller. Everyone is expected to "volunteer" at certain times for work that has to be done, be it physical labor in the fields of a collective farm, be it the work of cleaning city streets of snow or sweeping the city parks, be it a clean-up campaign for the subways or highways or public recreation centers, be it the unloading of freight cars or some other work requiring heavy physical exertion. The project matters little, and men of all professions participate in the communal effort. Doctors, lawyers, engineers, professors, teachers, factory workers, office clerks, schoolchildren, housewives— all freely lend a working hand on such occasions.

Nobody refuses, nobody feels in the least belittled by participating in such organized work drives. Instead, each feels content and even somewhat proud to do his bit for the creation of a better society. Yes, a lot of the talk on such occasions is simply rhetoric and lip service; but a lot of it is not. There is a pride that the ordinary Soviet citizen feels in being part of a society that has made tremendous gains—industrially, economically, educationally, scientifically, socially, and perhaps culturally—in the past generation, a nation that has risen from the ashes and the rubble of war to become one of the two recognized world superpowers. Of course people will grumble and grouse about the price they have had to pay, about the lack of consumer goods, about the years of hardship and sacrifice. Yet by the same token they can be, and are, proud of the sacrifices they have made, and so can take credit thereby for the society that has been built by their sacrifices.

There was none of that spirit among the prisoners of the Siberian camps, even though we did manage in the years I spent there to build whole towns, construct huge factory complexes, open up and work new mines, and complete all the facilities necessary to turn a frozen, barren wilderness into a functioning and productive center of industry. And we did it while living in the most primitive conditions, fed at starvation levels, without any but the most essential tools. We did it by forced labor, brute strength, and sheer weight of numbers. We did it not out of any sense of challenge or pioneering, but as a punishment and because we had to work if we wanted to go on living. But we did it. The industrialization of the Far North is now a reality, thanks to the convict labor of literally millions of men. Yet the only sense of satisfaction these driven, hungry, exhausted men ever had in all those terrible labors was the satisfaction each individual took in surviving just one more day. And for those who survived to the end, *that* was their achievement—not the buildings, not the tamed wilderness, not the construction they left behind, but the fact that they had survived to walk away from it.

In all the years I served in the Siberian camps, with few exceptions, I was assigned to the lowest work and the roughest brigades. That was my lot because of the charges on which I had been convicted. Moreover, the camps gave me an opportunity to work again in some fashion as a priest, and I took full advantage of it. The camp officials knew all about such activities through informers, and insisted that I stop. When I refused, when I continued to minister to my fellow prisoners, I was punished by being assigned to rough brigades, to the hardest types of labor, to extra heavy duty that would drive me to near exhaustion and leave me little time or energy to function as a priest. No efforts of influential friends or sympathizers ever succeeded in getting me transferred to a better brigade, except on rare occasions and for short periods of time. Through all the years in Siberia, my fortune was to belong to the lowest brigades doing the dirtiest work, digging foundations by hand, carving out with pick and shovel through the frozen ground long sewer trenches, loading and unloading with my bare hands and brute strength the heavy construction materials, crawling in the damp, dark holes of new mines, where death was always one careless step or an accident away.

So I came, during all those years, to know work at its worst—at its most brutal, its most degrading, its most dehumanizing worst. And I reflected a lot about it, as I said; I thought a lot about it and I prayed much over it. What was work to me during those years, if not a punishment, if not a curse? Truly, "in the sweat of my brow did I eat my bread", and little enough bread at that. What was there ennobling about my work? I didn't even have the satisfaction a father and mother can feel, worn out by work as they may be, in having provided food and a modicum of comfort for their family. I couldn't feel the sense of challenge, of self-sacrifice, of patriotism a Soviet citizen might feel who had volunteered to work for a year or two in the "virgin lands", leaving behind a family and all that was dear to him to travel to the arctic in order to help build a factory, open a new mine, or complete a housing project. And even my work itself offered little in which I could take pride or satisfaction: it was the lowest, the commonest, the roughest labor, requiring no skill or thought, "just a strong back and a weak mind", as we used to say.

And yet I did take pride in it. I did each job as best I could. I worked to the limit of my strength each day and did as much as my health and endurance under the circumstances made possible. Why? Because I saw this work as the will of God for me. I didn't build a new city in Siberia because Joseph Stalin or Nikita Khruschchev wanted it, but because God wanted it. The labor I did was not a punishment, but a way of working out my salvation in fear and trembling. Work was not a curse, even the brutish grunt work I was doing, but a way to God—and perhaps even a way to help others to God. I could not, therefore, look upon this work as degrading; it was ennobling, for it came to me from the hand of God himself. It was his will for me.

My fellow prisoners, of course, were quick to ask me if I was crazy. They could understand a man working to overfulfill a quota if it meant more food, but not out of a sense of pride or accomplishment. My strength and my limited endurance after years in prison rarely made it possible for me to do much more than make my daily quota, not overfulfill it, so they could not understand why I drove myself so hard and did my best each day. They asked me how I could possibly cooperate with the wishes of the government, why I always did my best instead of sabotaging the work, how I could help to build a new society for the communists, who rejected God and despised everything I stood for. Christian prisoners, indeed, even asked me if it were not sinful to cooperate with, or at least give the appearance of cooperating with, communism.

I tried to explain that the pride I took in my work differed from the pride a communist might take in building up the new society. The difference lay in the motivation. As a Christian, I could share in their concern for building a better world. I could work as hard as they for the common good. The people who would benefit from my labors would be just that: people. Human beings. Families in need of shelter against the arctic weather of Norilsk, or people in far-off places elsewhere who would have a better life because of the natural resources I had helped to liberate from this frozen earth or because of the materials which the factories I helped build would someday produce. I could justify, therefore, my cooperation in this work for the good of all mankind if it came to that; it differed little in that respect from any work any man anywhere might undertake. But there was more to it than that; there was the realization that work of itself is not a curse but a sharing in God's own work of creation, a redemptive and redeeming act, noble of itself and worthy of the best in man—even as it was worthy of God himself.

There is a tremendous truth contained in the realization that when God became man he became a workingman. Not a king, not a chieftain, not a warrior or a statesman or a great leader of nations, as some had thought the Messiah would be. The Gospels show us Christ the teacher, the healer, the wonder-worker, but these activities of his public life were the work of three short years. For all the rest of the time of his life on earth, God was a village carpenter and the son of a carpenter. He did not fashion benches or tables or beds or roof beams or plowbeams by means of miracles, but by hammer and saw, by ax and adz. He worked long hours to help his father, and then became the support of his widowed mother, by the rough work of a hill country craftsman. Nothing he worked on, as far as we know, ever set any fashions or became a collector's item. He worked in a shop every day, week in and week out, for some twenty years. He did the work all of us have to do in our lifetimes. There was nothing spectacular about it, there was much of the routine about it, perhaps much that was boring. There is little we can say about the jobs we do or have done that could not be said of the work God himself did when he became a man.

Yet he did not think it demeaning, beneath his dignity, dehumanizing. If anything, he restored to man's work its original dignity, its essential function as a share in God's creative act. Once again God worked, and on the seventh day he rested. For our Lord, though, it was not merely a symbolic action like that of the politician who sweeps one section of a sidewalk to launch a cleanup campaign or turns the first spadeful of earth at a ground-breaking ceremony. He worked day in and day out for some twenty years to set us an example, to show us that these routine chores, too, are not beneath man's dignity or even God's dignity, that simple household tasks and the repetitious work of the wage earner are not necessary evils but noble and redemptive works worthy of God himself. Work cannot be a curse if God himself undertook it; to eat one's bread in the sweat of one's brow is to do nothing more or less than Christ himself did. And he did it for a reason. He did it for years on end, he did it for more than three quarters of his life on earth, to convince us that God has not asked of us anything more tedious, more tiring, more routine and humdrum, more unspectacular than God himself has done. He did it to make it plain that the plainest and dullest of jobs is—or at any rate can be, if viewed properly in respect to God and to eternity—a sharing in the divine work of creation and redemption, a daily opportunity to cooperate with God in the central acts of his covenant of salvation.

For me as a priest, the thought of Christ the carpenter, Christ the workingman, was motivation enough. I could work again as a priest, now, in the camps—but that was not the only work God had sent me to do. "I have given you an example", he said to his disciples at the Last Supper, "that as I have ministered to you so also you must minister to one another". My ministry did not consist solely in teaching, in healing, in administering the sacraments —no more than his life on earth had consisted only of the three years of his public life. I was set here in the midst of the labor camps to work as he might have worked if he had been here, to set the example of work he would set if he were in my place. For I was Christ in this prison camp. And part of my teaching had to be that work, all work, any work, has a value in itself. It has a value insofar as it partakes in the creative act of God. It has a value insofar as it partakes of God's redemptive acts. It has a value in itself and a value for others.

Through it I worked out not only my own salvation—by accepting the situations of each day as from the hand of God and laboring so that I might offer them back to him somehow improved by my efforts—but also for the salvation of others, at least by the example I could set for them. Beyond that, I could offer up my labors, my hardships, as a redemptive act for others and as a means of reparation and atonement for my own past failings as well as theirs. In the cruel circumstances of the camps, where men had lost all sense and understanding of the dignity of work, I as a priest had to serve as another Christ. By the way I went about my work, every day, every hour, to the best of my ability and the last ounce of my strength, I had to try to demonstrate again in the wind and snow and wilderness of Siberia what Christ had demonstrated through twenty years of carpentry at Nazareth: that work is not a curse but a gift of God, the very same gift he gave to the first man, Adam, when he created him in his own image and put him in the Garden of Eden to till it and keep it as the steward of the Lord.

Chapter Eleven

THE PRIESTHOOD

For all the hardships and suffering endured there, the prison camps of Siberia held one great consolation for me: I was able to function as a priest again. I was able to say Mass again, although in secret, to hear confessions, to baptize, to comfort the sick, and to minister to the dying. I was able to speak to others about God and instruct them in the faith, to strengthen those whose faith was weak, to help and enlighten those who were believers in name only but who wanted to be more, who might have said with that man in the Gospel, "Lord, I believe; help my unbelief."

Of course all this could not be done too openly. The authorities in the camps did more than simply frown on such priestly activities. Officially, of course, they were against religion and had the power of the law and the Soviet Constitution, which forbade proselytizing, on their side. But there was more to their opposition than that. They knew priests had influence on other people. From the point of view of those in charge of the camps, therefore, that made priests especially dangerous no matter what they were telling their fellow prisoners. Accordingly, priests were called in regularly for interviews by the NKVD security agents. I had my share of such interviews. One purpose of the interviews was a sort of constant psychological warfare, a form of harassment and intimidation, a not so gentle reminder that such dangerous enemies of the Soviet people as priests were constantly under surveillance.

From time to time in these interviews, the security agents would deliberately let it be known that much of the priests' activities were immediately known to them through informers.

The camps were full of informers, everybody knew that. Prisoners who worked in the camp offices frequently suspected or even knew for a fact who the informers were and would tip off their friends not to have anything to do with such men. Some informers were beaten up in retaliation; I knew of cases where they were even killed. But by and large the prisoners took it for granted that such people had simply caved in under whatever pressure the NKVD had used against them; it was a fact of life, and a man's first duty was to survive. So fellow prisoners might feel sorry for the man or they might hold him in contempt, but as a practical matter they simply avoided him or talked about nothing with him except the most ordinary things. In so close-knit a society as the prison camp, it did not take long for word to get around about who had joined the ranks of the informers. They made it easier for the other prisoners, in one sense, but it also served the authorities' purpose as well. It generated a feeling of mistrust among the prisoners; a man was really afraid to confide in anyone unless he knew him exceptionally well. And that made it all the more difficult for any sort of organization or conspiracy to come into being among the prisoners.

In the same way and for much the same reasons, I'm sure the security agents let it be known that informers were constantly watching priests, so that a man would be very slow to engage in religious conversation with an ever widening circle of people he did not know well. Another purpose of these frequent security interviews with priests was to find out just what the prisoners *were* saying. If they were not talking to priests about religion, they must be talking to them about something besides the weather. So the NKVD men would try to find out what was being said in the camp, who were the ringleaders of various groups, what was said privately in the barracks, how the prisoners felt about the regime, the system, the future. I consistently refused to cooperate in any such line of questioning; I had had a bellyful of cooperation with the NKVD in Lubianka. More than that, I felt I had to be extremely careful about giving even the external appearance of cooperating, lest there be any suspicion among the prisoners about placing the seal of confession in jeopardy. Of course there was never any question about that in my mind, but I had to be especially careful so no one else would have such doubts either.

I was punished for my lack of cooperation in these sessions in many ways. I was assigned to the lowest work brigades and even to the penal brigades, so that it would be impossible for me to build up an apostolic following. My brigades were changed frequently, my food rations were cut. I was assigned to the poorest barracks, allowed no privileges, not even the ones I might have earned. And if the brigadier or the man in charge of the barracks put my name on a list of privileges for some reason or other, there would quickly be intervention by some higher official to prevent my actually receiving it. Meanwhile, the harassment and the interviews went on.

There was no doubt that priests were singled out in this regard. But a system based on fear and intimidation, as the prison camps were, could not confine itself just to this religious minority. Camp officials were deathly afraid of and constantly on guard against little insurrections or revolts among the prisoners. They went to great lengths to break up nationality groups among the prisoners, or language groups, or even people from the same town or other common background, i.e., those who had been to universities or were former party members. Since the prison camps of the arctic circle, however, included men from all nationalities in the Soviet Union and many men with common backgrounds such as the army, the university, or the party, it was impossible for the security agents to prevent common interest groups from forming or associating with one another in non-working hours. No doubt that was one reason the working hours were stretched almost to the limits of human endurance. It was the reason for the creation of mixed brigades, where the prisoners shared little or no common interest. It was the reason why brigades were changed frequently. And finally, it was the reason why no secret was made of the use of informers by the security organs. At all costs, they had to be able to isolate potential troublemakers or leaders of any sort. And it was because of this potential for leadership among the nationality or religious groups that they singled out priests for surveillance as much as for any reasons of atheistic propaganda or anti-religious persecution.

Nevertheless, the amazing thing to me was how little all these security measures affected a priest's relations with other prisoners. The moment he appeared on the camp grounds by himself or with a fellow priest, he would be joined by passing prisoners. The moment it became known in a new brigade or a new barracks or a new camp that a man was a priest, he would be sought out. He didn't have to make friends; they came to him instead. It was a very humbling experience, because you quickly came to appreciate that it was God's grace at work and had little to do with your own efforts. People came to you because you were a priest, not because of what you were personally. They didn't always come, either, expecting wise counsel or spiritual wisdom or an answer to every difficulty; they came expecting absolution from their sins, the power of the sacrament. To realize this was a matter of joy and of humility. You realized that they came to you as a man of God, a representative of God, a man chosen from among men and ordained for men in the things that are of God; you realized, too, that this imposed upon you an obligation of service, of ministry, with no thought of personal inconvenience, no matter how tired you might be physically or what risks you might be running in the face of official threats. For my part, I could not help but see in every encounter with every prisoner the will of God for me, now, at this time and in this place, and the hand of providence that had brought me here by strange and torturous paths.

It was not always a matter of preaching God and religion. It was enough at times simply to respect each of your fellowmen in the camp, to do good to each no matter what he himself did or said, no matter how he acted toward you. Even the Christians who came specifically to seek advice needed sympathy and moral support more than they needed a reminder of their obligations or their failings. There was little call to preach about sin or damnation or hellfire to men who experience daily the hell of loneliness and separation and anxiety. A great deal of tolerance and a great deal of understanding were required of a priest if he wished to be effective among these unfortunate and almost degraded human beings. Common sense and intuition, a feeling for the finger of God's grace behind a question or a conversation or an encounter, was much more necessary than textbook answers in theology. Before my own sad experiences in Lubianka, where I finally came to understand that everything depends on God and not on self in matters spiritual, I had always thought I had a definite answer and an explanation for all the moral questions in every problem of conscience. Having failed the test myself, however, having learned God's truth the hard way, I was able in the camps to be of humble service to the men God sent my way each day. We come to know the workings of the spirit in ourselves slowly. How much more slowly, then, do we begin to detect the workings of that same spirit in others? As I worked daily in the camps, I thanked God over and over again for the awful period of purification I underwent in Lubianka so that I could serve these tortured men, and I thanked him, too, for the mysterious workings of his providence that had brought me here. But above all I thanked him for having chosen me to be a priest and for the joy he gave me now in being able to function as a priest again.

In every camp there were a number of priests. This, too, was a source of consolation to me. The ones who had been there the longest were usually the ones who had made the contacts necessary to obtain what we needed for Mass. They were delighted to have another priest in the camp, and quick to spread the word among the prisoners. Such friendship was a joy in itself, but it also meant a chance to go to confession and the sacraments again, to talk of spiritual things, to share experiences. We discussed together how best to answer the problems that the prisoners brought to us, problems peculiar to a prison camp and never covered in a course of theology. We exhorted and encouraged one another, shared prayers and short homilies. They may not have been the most polished sermons, but they were often moving and most provocative because of the circumstances under which they were delivered. It was something just to be with these men, and to see them prove in word and in deed their dedication to God and to the flock he entrusted to them day after day.

Not that all of them were perfect. Indeed, there were even

informers among the priests themselves. We sometimes knew it because trusted prisoners who worked in the offices would tell us of encounters they had seen. Sometimes these priests themselves would tell us privately how they had been pressured into such cooperation, and they begged our forgiveness. Strange as it may seem, these informers or suspected informers were never excluded from our company. They shared in our Masses. We heard their confessions and they heard ours; such was the power of our confidence in the seal of the confessional. And we could not bring ourselves to turn anyone away from the grace to be gained in the sacraments or in listening to the word of God. We all had our failings; each of us knew only too well how much we depended upon God and on his grace.

Every camp also had a number of Baptist ministers, but they would rarely have anything to do with us. Most of them, in fact, were fiercely anti-Catholic, at times openly antagonistic and hostile. They and their followers were usually a close-knit group. They held regular prayer meetings, recited the Bible from memory, and instructed each other to be faithful to Christ while opposing anti-Christ—whether in the guise of communism or Catholicism. Perhaps because they were so staunch and outspoken, or maybe simply because they were such a close-knit group, the camp officials were particularly severe on the Baptists and did their best to break up such groups. I was saddened and frequently puzzled at their attitude toward other believers, especially under the circumstances, yet one could not help but admire their dedication and the Christian witness they gave to their beliefs. There were some who felt that their relations with other Christians were not particularly Christlike or even charitable; yet if they sincerely believed the Church somehow stood for anti-Christ, one could perhaps understand their fear of us and their reactions. Certainly, in all other ways they were admirable; and they were never afraid to stand up for their faith, to suffer for it, and so give testimony in their daily lives to their religious beliefs.

The same could be said of the few Orthodox priests and monks I met in the prison camps. They were not very active, for the most part, but they seemed genuinely holy men. They stayed away from controversy or even much in the way of public religious activity; instead, they led a simple life of prayer and work. In the barracks they kept to themselves, rarely speaking to the other prisoners. Some older prisoners, themselves Orthodox, visited them occasionally and spent some time with them in private conversation, but they seemed to want to avoid doing anything that would call attention to themselves or that would get them into trouble with camp authorities. Nevertheless, the other prisoners showed respect for them, left them alone, and wondered sometimes at their life of prayer.

The key word, in fact, of our priestly apostolate in the camps had to be the word "witness". It was not so much a matter of preaching God and talking religion to the men around you as it was a matter of living the faith that you yourself professed. Many of them could not at first understand a life dedicated to God in work, in suffering, and in sacrifice. But they began by respecting it, and from that respect grew a sense of admiration and then of inquiry. It was not so much what you said, but what you did, how you lived, that influenced them. They were wise in the ways of the prison camp and the prison system; they knew that priests were the object of special harassment by the officials. Yet they saw these same priests refuse to become embittered, they saw them spend themselves in helping others, they saw them daily give of themselves beyond what was required without complaint, without thinking of themselves first, without regard for their own comfort or even safety. They saw them make themselves available to the sick and to the sinning, even to those who had abused or despised them. If a priest showed concern for such people, they would say, he must believe in something that makes him human and close to God at the same time. This quality in a priest was what appealed most to them. And it was this quality that led them to seek a new relationship with God by reconciling themselves to his laws and to conscience. To help prisoners return to a belief in God they had long abandoned or simply ignored for many years was our greatest joy and consolation.

The Catholics of Polish, Ukrainian, Lithuanian, and Latvian descent were the primary objects of our apostolate and the nucleus of any prison camp "parishes". They held steadfastly to the faith and were overjoyed to have a priest among them, to be able again to receive the sacraments. They traditionally held a priest in great respect, and in the camps they did whatever they could to care for us, to shield us, to make our apostolate possible and effective. They shared with us the little extra food they had. They stood on watch when we celebrated Mass, to warn us against the approach of the guards or the presence of informers. And they brought other prisoners to us. Not all of them were the most exemplary Christians, of course, but they were believers. They might not always be able to explain the truths of the faith in a way to satisfy the curiosity of those who had grown up in the Soviet system and heard religion ridiculed or explained away in the schools, but they were witnesses by their own faith to the fact that faith itself gave another dimension to life, that a man could believe in something beyond the material world and that this belief gave meaning and purpose to a life lived in circumstances that otherwise would be cause only for despair. It was through their belief, however imperfectly expressed, that others came to us to find out more about a faith that could give such meaning to their lives.

There were no startling conversions, no miracles performed, no sensational prayer sessions testifying to the working of the Holy Spirit, no pomp, no splendor in our religious services that could draw the curious minds of the ordinary worker to participate, no religious pretense whatsoever, for all our get-togethers for the Eucharist or any spiritual services were held in seclusion out of fear of repression. The little that was done, the simple way it was done for God—be it a clandestine Mass, a baptism, an office of the dead, a sermon preached on the spur of the moment, a sick call made, a confession heard, a mumbled word of advice or prayer while walking about the camp or marching through the snows to work, everything done in a deep spirit of faith—was the mission of the priest and the faithful alike in the prison camps. On the one hand, the priest never lost sight of his own insignificance. As a laborer in this vineyard, he sensed the seeming impossibility of ever influencing in any significant way the masses of people living in a professedly atheistic state. On the other hand, he could daily feel the power of God's grace, could trust completely in his divine providence. His task, therefore, was to do what was asked of him each day as perfectly as he could and leave the rest to God.

Being a priest also gave new purpose and meaning to the harsh labors and cruel sufferings men had to endure in order to survive the labor camps in Siberia. In his role as another Christ, as a mediator between God and men, the priest could offer up his suffering and his labors for his fellowmen. He could accept the works and sufferings of each day from God's hands and offer them back to God, not for himself alone but for all those around him who were struggling to keep the faith or had not yet received the gift of faith. It didn't make getting up in the morning to face another day of rough and wind-whipped work any easier, or the work itself any less exhausting, but it added a dimension of expiation and sacrifice to our lives beyond the sheer necessity of survival and enduring one more day. It gave another sense of purpose and of dedication to the priesthood; it added a sacramental element to the labor and the sufferings of the day. It made of every moment and of every effort a priestly work. For a priest is ordained to do more than simply celebrate the Mass or hear confessions, to console the sick and comfort the dying, to offer words of consolation and spiritual wisdom to those in need. "Every priest is chosen from among men and ordained to minister to men in those things that are of God", says the ordination ceremony. And the things that are of God are all the joys and works and sufferings of each day, however burdensome and boring, routine and insignificant they may seem. It is the priest's function to offer these things back to God for his fellowmen and to serve as an example, a witness, a martyr, a testimony before the men around him of God's providence and purpose. After all the years of isolation and loneliness in Lubianka, it was a joy for me to be able to do that once again amid the physical pain and suffering, the sorrow and despair, of the prison camps of arctic Siberia.

Chapter Twelve

THE APOSTOLATE

My aim in entering Russia was the same from beginning to end: to help people find God and attain eternal life. How the work of saving souls would develop, what form it would take, remained vague from the outset. Yet I was not troubled by this vagueness, for underlying whatever shaky visions of the future I had then was the certitude of faith and complete confidence in the workings of divine providence. I was always convinced, through twenty-three years in the Soviet Union, that God wanted me there; and whatever I did—significant or not—somehow confirmed my belief, my confidence, in his will. The thought that I was doing his will, trying to fulfill whatever he demanded of me each day, gave me that confidence. No evil could touch me, ultimately, as long as God was with me. How simple that sounds as I write it, even as it seemed simple then. Yet it is no less true for all its terrible simplicity, just as all great truths somehow seem to come out childishly or naïvely simple when we try to state them in stock formulas. Faith in God's reality and in his providence, for example, is what underlies the catechism statement "Man was created to praise, reverence, and serve God and by this means to save his soul." Yet that is the great truth behind all human existence.

At the beginning, too, I had only a vague awareness of the pain and suffering I would meet during my days in the Soviet Union. If anyone asked me whether I would be willing to suffer and die for the faith, I would have said, "Yes", I suppose. Such things are easy to say when the threat is vague and faith is strong. In all honesty, I never really gave much thought to the hardships I would face in Russia. I found it easy to say, "Father, into your hands I commend my spirit", and to trust that God would protect me as long as I did my best in following his will. I never stopped to reflect, then, that those words of Christ had been uttered in his final agony on the cross, as a conclusion to his passion and his work on earth.

Pain and suffering are something we all prefer not to think about, something we would sooner avoid. I remember that even as a boy I used to hate sermons or retreat talks about our Lord's passion. When teachers or retreat masters would picture the agonies Christ underwent, I used to shudder. It all seemed so vivid and yet so useless; there seemed to be no sense in it. The thought of pain repelled me, whether in the passion or in life around me; life to me was something much too precious to distort by pain. So I wanted to hear something else about the passion other than the pain, I looked for some other significance to Christ's suffering. I think I first began to find it in the lumber camps of the Ural Mountains with the pain and suffering, both physical and spiritual, I encountered there. Because it was there that I first began to understand pain and suffering in the larger context of an apostolate.

Had I come to Russia because I wanted it? No, I came because I was convinced God wanted me there. And my coming, my following of the will of God, had meant sacrifices. It had meant leaving behind my own country, the Jesuits I had known and worked with, my family and friends, and everything that had been familiar to me in the first thirty years of my life. In a word, it had meant breaking with all I had known and done before, in order to adapt myself to an entirely new, strange, difficult, and strenuous life of hardship in which to carry on an apostolate. It is the same sacrifice demanded of and made by so many people· missionaries, servicemen, married couples, young people leaving home for the first time. Such sacrifice is the first test of any vocation, any calling to follow God's will. "In the head of the book it is written of me," the prophets had said of Christ, "I come to do your will." That was to be the keynote of his life and of his vocation, as it is the keynote of every Christian vocation, and it was only in the light of that faithfulness to the Father's will through sacrifice and pain and suffering that one should hear

Christ's words on the cross, "Father, into your hands I commend my spirit."

But why the passion? Why pain and suffering? Is God so vindictive that he must inflict pain and suffering on those who follow him? The answer lies not in God's will but in the world in which we live and try to follow his will. Christ's life and suffering were redemptive; his "apostolate" in the scheme of salvation was to restore the original order and harmony in all creation that had been destroyed by sin. His perfect obedience to the Father's will redeemed man's first and continuing disobedience to that will. "All creation", said St. Paul, "groans and labors up till now," awaiting Christ's redemptive efforts to restore the proper relationship between God and his creation. But Christ's redemptive act did not of itself restore all things; it simply made the work of redemption possible, it began our redemption. Just as all men share in the disobedience of Adam, so all men must share in the obedience of Christ to the Father's will. Redemption will be complete only when all men share his obedience. So the world has not been changed overnight, and it is the world in which we seek to follow Christ's example that afflicts us as it afflicted him. It is not the Father, not God, who inflicts suffering upon us but rather the unredeemed world in which we must labor to do his will, the world in whose redemption we must share.

It was in the lumber camps of the Ural Mountains that the Polish and Jewish refugees with whom I came to work first rebuked me for the way I lived, for the conscientious way I went about my work. "What are you working for?" they would ask. "What are you out to prove?" I knew they couldn't understand why I worked so hard, why I should suffer hunger and hardship, working all day in a half-frozen river or out in a snow-covered forest, standing in line for hours to get extra bread, enduring sleepless nights, putting up with inadequate housing and tattered clothes. It meant nothing to them for me to speak of an apostolate, for me to say that I did it just to be with them, to be available to them under the urging of God's will. And yet that was the truth of it. From a purely human standpoint, my sojourn in the Soviet Union could have been considered the most stupid and senseless action of my life. But I saw these hardships, this drab reality, as an integral part of my apostolate. I could not separate this earthly reality from the will of God, because the will of God has to be worked out by each of us here on earth.

The spiritual pain and suffering, even more than the physical pain and suffering, increased during my five years of interrogations. There were times then when I nearly lost sight of my purpose in the agony of self-doubt, the anguish I felt when tempted to believe I had been abandoned by God. Afterwards, in the camps, it was easier once more to put all the aches and pains, the sufferings and shortcomings and discouragements, into the context of the apostolate. It was then I could reflect on how unimportant my efforts were in saving souls if conceived of apart from God's will. The thought that actions otherwise worthless in themselves could be somehow redemptive, could serve the growth of his kingdom upon earth because they were undertaken in obedience to his will, and that such actions could even be the source of grace for others, could share in Christ's work of meriting grace for all—that thought sustained me in joy and drove me on to work ever harder to achieve more perfect communion with God and his will.

This simple truth, that the sole purpose of man's life on earth is to do the will of God, contains in it riches and resources enough for a lifetime. Once you have learned to live with it uppermost in mind, to see each day and each day's activities in its light, it becomes more than a source of eternal salvation; it becomes a source of joy and happiness here on earth. The notion that the human will, when united with the divine will, can play a part in Christ's work of redeeming all mankind is overpowering. The wonder of God's grace transforming worthless human actions into efficient means for spreading the kingdom of God here on earth astounds the mind and humbles it to the utmost, yet brings a peace and joy unknown to those who have never experienced it, unexplainable to those who will not believe.

In this subtle insight of the soul touched by God's divine power lies the root of true interior joy. And as long as this vision persists, as long as the soul does not lose sight of this great truth, the inner joy and peace that follow upon it persist through even the saddest and gravest moments of human trial and suffering. Pain and suffering do not thereby cease to exist; the ache and anguish of body and soul do not vanish from man's consciousness. But even they become a means of nourishing this joy, of fostering peace and conformity to God's will, for they are seen as a continuation of Christ's passion—not in the distorted, senseless acts of bloody butchery I had shuddered over as a boy, but as purposeful, redemptive, healing acts by which the world is reconciled to the will of the Father. Such suffering can only bring with it deep spiritual joy, for from it springs redemption and salvation, the ultimate victory over sin and further suffering and even death itself. By man's first disobedience, says St. Paul, sin entered the world, and through sin, death. And only by man's obedience, by conformity to the will of God, will sin be eliminated and so suffering and death.

Consoling as conformity to the will of God may be for the soul, as productive of peace and joy as it may prove, it cannot be gained simply for the asking. Nor, in my opinion, can a proper understanding of pain and suffering be achieved without the larger vision of salvation or the more immediate context of apostolate and of vocation. For my part, at any rate, I learned it only through the constant practice of prayer, by trying to live always in the presence of God, by trying to see all things as a manifestation of his divine will. It wasn't always easy, nor did I always succeed. Through the hardships of the Urals, through the anguish of Lubianka, through the sufferings and adversities of the prison camps, my inner struggle of soul never ceased. No matter how close to God the soul felt, how blessed it was by an awareness of his presence on occasion, the realities of life were always at hand, always demanding recognition, always demanding acceptance. I had continuously to learn to accept God's will—not as I wished it to be, not as it might have been, but as it actually was at the moment. And it was through the struggle to do this that spiritual growth and a greater appreciation of his will took place.

Of course there were doubts, at one time there was near despair. It was not reason that sustained me then but faith. Only by faith could I find God present in every circumstance, only by faith could I penetrate the mystery of his saving grace, not by questioning it in any way but by fully cooperating with it in exactly the way he asked. It was then, in differing measures and with varying degrees of success, that the glimpses of his providence ruling all things would work to dispel the doubts and the fears that were constantly on the edges of the mind. So I learned by trial and error that if I wanted to preserve my interior peace and joy I had to have constant recourse to prayer, to the eyes of faith, to a humility that could make me aware of how little my own efforts meant and how dependent I was upon God's grace even for prayer and faith itself.

None of this came easily, for I was not a disembodied spirit. Hunger could distract me, the interrogators could confuse me, a body aching in every joint and worn down by a long arctic day of grueling work could leave me totally exhausted and very much discouraged. It is much easier to see the redemptive role of pain and suffering in God's plan if you are not actually undergoing pain and suffering. It was only by struggling with such feelings, however, that growth occurred. Each victory over discouragement gave an increase in spiritual courage; every success, however fleeting, in finding the hand of God behind all things, made it easier to recapture the sense of his purpose in a new day of seemingly senseless work and hardship and suffering.

Day by day, I learned to experience in some measure the power of God as manifested in the mystery of the passion. Pain and suffering comprised the sacrifice needed in the passion for saving souls. A similar sacrifice had to be undertaken by all those called to the apostolate. And yet the suffering and sacrifice were touched by deep spiritual joy, because in them one saw God's will accomplished in an otherwise frustrating life, the great work of salvation promoted. If you look upon sacrifice and suffering only through the eyes of reason alone, your tendency will be to avoid as much of it as you can, for pain in itself is never pleasant. But if you can learn to see the role of pain and suffering in relation to God's redemptive plan for the universe and each individual soul, your attitude must change. You don't shun it when it comes upon you, but bear it in the measure grace is given you. You see in it a putting on of Christ in the true sense of the word. Out of this insight comes joy, and an increase of hope; out of it, too, grows compassion for others and a hope that they also may be helped to understand the true meaning of life and its trials, its joys and its sufferings. Fired with this enthusiasm, the soul constantly yearned to communicate the wonders of God's grace to everyone. This desire, this zeal, knew no bounds, set no limits for its activity. Though its attainment in reality was something that surpassed human effort, the soul on fire with this understanding paid little attention to concrete results. The most important thing was to keep the flame of zeal burning. Hence the constant need of daily prayer, the constant efforts to see in the pain and suffering of each day a true work of redemption, a true sharing in the saving acts of Christ.

The obstacles met with each day, the difficulties encountered in putting such zeal into practice, did not upset a soul on fire with this realization. For the actual conversion of people required much prayer, much persevering trust in God, many trials and sacrifices. The dedicated soul instinctively realized, in constant communion with God, that what was most important in the Father's eyes was total surrender to his will in the apostolate. Whatever he inspired or commanded became paramount, not the human effort or the wisdom or the work resulting from personal initiative.

Reflecting on such thoughts almost habitually, amid the exhausting labors of endless days in the camps of Siberia, made me conscious of my obligation toward God in fulfilling to the best of my abilities the daily rounds of prayer and work and suffering, setting an example as conscientiously as I could for my fellow prisoners, helping them to see by word and by deed that even the days of this most wretched existence in a frozen wasteland could be productive in bringing the kingdom of God upon earth. No man's life, no man's suffering, is lost from the eyes of God. For each of us has been created to praise, reverence, and serve God and by this means to save our souls and help in the salvation of others. No action, however insignificant, if accepted and performed as from God's hand and in conformity with his will, is anything other than redemptive and a sharing in the great work of salvation begun by Christ's passion.

Reflecting on these truths was consoling, but it was more than that. It opened up to me a whole new vision of Siberia and the pain and suffering that went on around me. It seemed to me that I could see arising out of the devastated and blighted lives around me, a whole new Church to come—if only there were laborers enough for the vineyard. A Church of men and women full of sacrifice and total dedication was in the process of formation here. A Church formed out of a generation of persecution and frustration, tried as gold in the furnace. A Church of new leaders, survivors of these camps and living in a militantly atheistic country, yet aware of how totally all things depended upon God alone, unable to worship publicly perhaps and yet united to the entire mystical body of Christ called the Church. That saving remnant, perhaps, of which Isaiah spoke. A people who accepted persecution with joy might see in their own trials and sufferings the true Christian work of redeeming the world about them, of being the leaven in the mass. "For who has known the mind of the Lord or who has been his counselor? My ways are not your ways, says the Lord; as far as the heavens are above the earth are my ways above your ways." Perhaps, in God's providence, there might result from all this suffering something new and precious in the mystical body: zealous Christians, with a new ideal of dedication to offer the Church existing in the world as a human institution. In God's providence, this Church under persecution—these suffering Christians—constantly enriched the Church upon earth, the mystical body of Christ.

Chapter Thirteen

THE MEANING OF THE MASS

Sometimes I think that those who have never been deprived of an opportunity to say or hear Mass do not really appreciate what a treasure the Mass is. I know, in any event, what it came to mean to me and the other priests I met in the Soviet Union; I know the sacrifices we made and the risks we ran in order just to have a chance to say or hear Mass. When we were constantly hungry in the camps, when the food we got each day was just barely enough to keep us going, I have seen priests pass up breakfast and work at hard labor on an empty stomach until noon in order to keep the Eucharistic fast, because the noon break at the work site was the time we could best get together for a hidden Mass. I did that often myself. And sometimes, when the guards were observing us too closely and we couldn't risk saying Mass at the work site, the crusts of bread I had put in my pocket at breakfast remained there uneaten until I could get back to camp and say Mass at night. Or again, during the long arctic summer, when the work days were the longest and our hours of sleep were at a minimum, I have seen priests and prisoners deprive their bodies of needed sleep in order to get up before the rising bell for a secret Mass in a quiet barracks, while everyone else clung to those precious extra moments of sleep. In some ways, we led a catacomb existence with our Masses. We would be severely punished if we were discovered saying Mass, and there were always informers. But the Mass to us was always worth the danger and the sacrifice; we treasured it, we looked forward to it, we would do almost anything in order to say or attend a Mass.

When I had been in Rome at the Russian college, dreaming of a chance to reach the Soviet Union, I had often wondered what I would do if I could not say Mass. Sometimes, as students, we talked about it. Rome, with its catacombs, probably served as inspiration for some of those conversations. But our speculations surely were somewhat romantic. We attended Mass every day at the Roman college, as we had done every day of our lives at the seminary and in our Jesuit houses; we prepared ourselves for ordination to say Mass in both the Oriental rite and the Latin rite. The Mass had a special meaning for us as future priests, but I suppose it would be true to say that we still took it for granted somehow. Not that it became just another religious ceremony; for me, at least, the Mass always had a special meaning as a time of particular intimacy with our Lord each day. But it was so easy to attend Mass each day. It was always there, a part of the daily order, and the thought that it might someday be difficult to be able to say Mass was really only a daydream. It was something you talked about, something you read about in the history of the Church persecutions, but not really something you had ever had to suffer or experience. I remember the thrill of my first Mass after the day of ordination, the privilege of performing with my own two hands the re-enactment of Calvary, my joy at the thought that I had been chosen from among men for the things that were of God and could at last fulfill the command Christ gave his disciples at the Last Supper: "Do this, in memory of me." From the day of ordination, through the quiet years at Albertyn and the turmoil and upheaval that followed the Soviet takeover of Poland, there was never a day that did not begin for me with the sacrifice of the Mass.

It was only when Father Victor and I began the long train ride from Lvov to the lumber camps of the Ural Mountains that our once idle daydreams about not being able to say Mass became a reality. It was only then that I first experienced the very real sense of deprivation at not being able to begin the day by celebrating the Eucharist. We carried with us bread and wine and a little Mass kit with a chalice and missal so we could say Mass. But no one in the boxcar full of workers knew we were priests, and in the crowded conditions of the car we found it very difficult to say

Mass. We did the best we could. At every opportunity, particularly at stops along the way when we would leave the boxcars to stretch our legs and forage for extra food, we seized our chance to celebrate the Eucharist together. When we reached the lumber camps and found ourselves faced with barracks life in the primitive, roughhewn quarters of the camps, we found it equally difficult to say Mass. We were afraid to risk exposure; we did not know how we would be accepted as priests and, at least in the beginning, we would only celebrate Mass when we were alone together. If we waited until we could go off into a quiet corner of the barracks during the evening, it meant that we must fast all day and still do a full day's work with the lumber gangs. Yet the barracks would be in a turmoil each morning as everyone prepared for work; it was hard to find the time then for the recollection we desired in order to celebrate Mass as we wanted. Accordingly, we did not manage to say Mass every day, but we kept a supply of consecrated hosts so we could at least go to Communion every day.

The danger and the difficulty of saying Mass became a reality for us in the lumber camps of the Urals. We began then to do what we probably should have done before: we began to prepare ourselves to say the Mass by heart. We were afraid we would lose our Mass kit, the chalice or the missal; but we were determined that as long as we had bread and wine we would try to say Mass somehow. Over and over again in the evenings, when others were chatting or reading or playing cards, we would repeat to each other the prayers of the Mass until we had learned them by heart. How often, in the years that followed, I thanked God for this interlude in the lumber camps of the Urals and the time of training and of grace that was given to me to prepare for the years ahead.

After a few months, when Father Victor and I had adjusted somewhat to barracks existence as a way of life, we were able to find more and more occasions to say Mass. We would walk out together, for example, into the forest and there offer Mass on a stump of a tree. I could not help thinking how the forests sometimes resembled a cathedral—the tall rows of towering trees arching over us, the hushed silence, the natural beauty around us, the silent whiteness of the snow in winter. Even time seemed to stand still as we offered the eternal sacrifice of Calvary for the many intentions that filled our thoughts and our hearts, not the least of which was the thought of the deprived thousands of the Church of silence here in this once Christian land for whom we had come to work as priests in secret. I shall never forget, as long as I am a priest, those Masses in the forests in the Urals.

At other times, Father Victor and I would say Mass sitting on the edge of our beds across from one another. We pretended to be reading or talking softly as we said the Mass prayers. We could not use the chalice in the barracks, so our cup became a common drinking glass and our host a piece of leavened bread. If people stopped to chat, we tried to break off conversation as pleasantly and as quickly as we could and so recapture our recollection and continue our secret Eucharist. I worked outside with the lumber gangs, but Father Victor worked as an accountant in the company offices, so he always kept the Blessed Sacrament wrapped in a purificator inside his wallet in the pocket of his coat. That way, we could at least receive Communion each day if Mass became impossible. Later on, after we had made friends with the scrub-woman who took care of the barracks, we would sometimes leave the Blessed Sacrament carefully hidden inside a bundle of clothes in her little private office and living room. She was a Catholic, as we came to know, and she helped us in many ways. It was one of her greatest joys to have the Blessed Sacrament in her room and to know that the Lord she worshiped dwelt under her roof.

You cannot explain all this, I know, to those who do not believe. Even for many Christians, I fear, the notion of the Blessed Sacrament as the bread of life is somehow only a poetic or symbolic phrase used by Jesus in the Gospel. Yet what a source of sustenance it was to us then, how much it meant to us to have the Body and Blood of Christ as the food of our spiritual lives in this sacrament of love and joy. The experience was very real; you could feel its effects upon your mind and heart, upon your daily life. For us it was a necessity, to foster the life of the soul, just as much as our daily bread was necessary to sustain the body. There were so many of the exiles here in the Urals who were deprived of it and seemed indifferent. God in his own way took care of these spiritually starved people, I have no doubt, just as he was taking care of us in a special way. Who of us can fully understand the ways of God? For us, though, this bread of life, this Eucharist, was truly a source of communion with him and with those to whom we longed to bring him.

The five long years in Lubianka brought this home to me more forcefully than ever. I was deprived of that spiritual food and the reality of that communion. I turned to God in prayer, made frequent acts of spiritual communion throughout the day, but I literally hungered to be able to receive him once again. Every day I said from memory the prayers of the Mass and sometimes I think these prayers served only to emphasize my sense of deprivation from the Eucharist. In those days of torment and stress, of darkness and humiliation, I knew I desperately needed that source of strength the bread of life might have provided—and I could not have it. I prayed to God, I talked to him and asked for help and strength, I knew that he was with me. All this I had, and yet I could not have him in my hands, I could not have his sacramental presence. And the difference to me was very real. It was a hunger of the soul as real to me as the bodily hunger I constantly experienced through those years. I have often wondered, in the years since, whether I would have failed as badly, have come so close to despair, if I had somehow had available to me that bread of life.

When I reached the prison camps of Siberia, I learned to my great joy that it was possible to say Mass daily once again. In every camp, the priests and prisoners would go to great lengths, run risks willingly, just to have the consolation of this sacrament. For those who could not get to Mass, we daily consecrated hosts and arranged for the distribution of Communion to those who wished to receive. Our risk of discovery, of course, was greater in the barracks, because of the lack of privacy and the presence of informers. Most often, therefore, we said our daily Mass somewhere at the work site during the noon break. Despite this added hardship, everyone observed a strict Eucharistic fast from the night before, passing up a chance for breakfast and working all morning on an empty stomach. Yet no one complained. In small groups the prisoners would shuffle into the assigned place, and there the priest would say Mass in his working clothes, unwashed, disheveled, bundled up against the cold. We said Mass in drafty storage shacks, or huddled in mud and slush in the corner of a building site foundation of an underground. The intensity of devotion of both priests and prisoners made up for everything; there were no altars, candles, bells, flowers, music, snow-white linens, stained glass or the warmth that even the simplest parish church could offer. Yet in these primitive conditions, the Mass brought you closer to God than anyone might conceivably imagine. The realization of what was happening on the board, box, or stone used in place of an altar penetrated deep into the soul. Distractions caused by the fear of discovery, which accompanied each saying of the Mass under such conditions, took nothing away from the effect that the tiny bit of bread and few drops of consecrated wine produced upon the soul.

Many a time, as I folded up the handkerchief on which the body of our Lord had lain, and dried the glass or tin cup used as a chalice, the feeling of having performed something tremendously valuable for the people of this Godless country was overpowering. Just the thought of having celebrated Mass here, in this spot, made my journey to the Soviet Union and the sufferings I endured seem totally worthwhile and necessary. No other inspiration could have deepened my faith more, could have given me spiritual courage in greater abundance, than the privilege of saying Mass for these poorest and most deprived members of Christ the Good Shepherd's flock. I was occasionally overcome with emotion for a moment as I thought of how he had found a way to follow and to feed these lost and straying sheep in this most desolate land, So I never let a day pass without saying Mass; it was my primary concern each new day. I would go to any length, suffer any inconvenience, run any risk to make the bread of life available to these men.

The bread and wine for Mass were smuggled in to us by the people of nearby arctic towns, but they generally came all the way from the Ukraine. It wasn't really possible to buy Mass wine in the Siberian stores, for all the wines available there contained impurities.

People who had themselves survived the camps and returned home to the Ukraine, however, would send a small wooden barrel of Mass wine, about four quarts, to friends they had made in the towns around the camps. These friends, with the help of some sympathetic truck driver who drove in and out of the fenced and guarded prison working zones to make deliveries of construction materials, would then manage to smuggle the wine in to a prisoner priest. There was, in fact, a regular traffic in smuggled goods into the camps. Vodka and foodstuffs were delivered in this way by free people in the towns who took pity on the prisoners, so it was not just Mass wine that reached us regularly. The night shift usually had a better chance of concealing the goods, for the night guards were frequently not as strict as the day guards; only skeleton crews of prisoners worked at night as maintenance men, so the guards were fewer and security much less tight.

Priests in the Ukraine or Poland or Lithuania who had not yet been arrested, or who had been released from the camps and returned home, made it a point to look after fellow priests serving terms in the camps. Nuns, too, worked marvels in helping prisoner priests. According to camp rules, a prisoner had the right to write his immediate family twice a year. Packages could also be received occasionally, when permission was granted to the prisoner by the chief of security; usually, two packages a year were the limit. Prisoner priests, therefore, informed their relatives where they were and hinted in their letters that the priests at home be told about them and about other priests who were with them. Since priests in the Ukraine and in occupied countries were under strict surveillance, though, it was generally the nuns who managed to look after the needs of deported, exiled, and imprisoned clergy. Many of them had managed to get work in local hospitals when their convents were closed, and it was they who supplied priests in the camps with Mass bread, wine, and Mass books. Pages of the books would be mixed up with newspaper and used as packing. Other pages of the missal would be used to wrap the Mass bread. The guards paid little attention to such "scrap paper" in the packages, but some pages of the books would naturally be lost or thrown into the wastebasket. Prisoners who worked as janitors in the offices would be alerted, therefore, to look for and save these discarded pages before they could be burned. For a promise of a portion of the package, hungry prisoners, whether Christians or not, were always willing to do this favor and so outwit camp authorities.

Wine was a little different problem, but the nuns sent the wine, as I have said, to designated people in nearby towns. Then, in various ways and through various people, small amounts of wine were smuggled into the camp. Even at the risk of being caught and punished, faithful prisoners willingly cooperated in helping us keep a supply of Mass bread and wine at various locations in the camp. As a result, every priest in the camp received what was needed to say Mass daily. If he needed something, he had only to ask and it was provided for him if at all possible. So even in the often impossible conditions of the prison camps, a priest who let it be known that he wanted to say Mass could always do so. And we did.

Within the camp, though, Mass could only be said if the greatest precautions were taken. Prisoners moved about constantly in the barracks; there were informers in every work brigade. To go to a barracks other than your own was strictly forbidden, and you would be asked to leave the minute someone noticed you didn't belong there. It wasn't just the guards who were so strict. The prisoners themselves took such precautions, because expert thieves were always on the lookout for a chance to steal something, anything that was better than what they had. If we got together outside the barracks, the guards became wary and suspicious of such small groups and ordered everyone to return to the barracks.

Saying Mass in the camp barracks was difficult and dangerous, and we attempted it only on rare occasions, or because of some urgent necessity. Then we would have to huddle together in a dark corner, while friendly prisoners stood watch in the corridors to warn us of the approach of the camp guards. At their signal we would hastily consume the species of consecrated bread and wine and quickly break up the group. Only once was I actually caught. Three guards, obviously directed by informers, came suddenly into the corner of the barracks where I was seated saying Mass

with a few companions, and made straight for us. They made us
get up and stand aside while they searched. They threw the
particles of consecrated bread onto the floor and under the bunks
amid all kinds of rubble. The consecrated wine, though, wasn't
touched, for alongside the tin cup used as a chalice there were
other tin cups standing on the stool we had been using as an altar.
Every priest at some time or other during his life in camp experienced the same sad business. It was distressing, to say the least, and
it made us worry about every Mass for fear of the same risk of
discovery and sacrilege.

Generally, therefore, we preferred to say Mass somewhere at
the working site, even though it meant we had to fast all morning
and then give up the few moments of rest allowed to prisoners
during the luncheon break. Even then, we could not invite many
people to attend the Mass lest a daily crowd in the same place
might draw attention to our activities. We usually chose a shack or
some corner of a foundation far from the current working areas—
sometimes it took fifteen minutes or more to reach the shack or
building where Mass was to be said—and we had to start on time
in order not to return late to our places of work. All of this made
it difficult to have many prisoners in attendance, so we would
consecrate extra bread and distribute Communion to the other
prisoners when we could. Sometimes that meant we would only
see them when we returned to the barracks at night before dinner.
Yet these men would actually fast all day long and do exhausting
physical labor without a bite to eat since dinner the evening
before, just to be able to receive the Holy Eucharist—that was
how much the sacrament meant to them in this otherwise God-
forsaken place.

Our rare free days, when all the prisoners were allowed to rest
in camp, were the hardest of all on which to say Mass. It was the
easiest time to say Mass for a large group, though, if we could get
together on some pretext or other in the prison camp yard, and
occasionally we did risk such a Mass, especially if the day coin-
cided with a special religious feast or festival. But generally on
such days I would say Mass early in the morning, half lying on the
bunk while most of the prisoners still slept. I would procure the

wine the night before in the camp clinic or the camp disinfecting room, where friends who worked there kept the wine hidden for the priests. I held the bread in my hands wrapped in a piece of white cloth as I lay on the bunk, and I said the prayers of the Mass by heart. Before the signal to rise was given, I would have finished my Mass on these occasions and then be able to distribute Communion to others under cover of the general commotion and moving about that always followed the rising signal. Time and again I was amazed at the devotion of these men. Most of them had really had very little formal religious training; for the most part they knew little of religion except the prayers and beliefs that pious parents or grandparents had taught them. And yet they believed, and were willing to make unheard-of sacrifices for the consolation of attending Mass or receiving Communion.

Christian prisoners in general showed great respect for the priests in camp. Most of their free time they sought to spend in their company. Even those who did not actively practice their faith often preferred to spend time in the group around a priest. They defended and supported and encouraged the priests as much as they could. Somehow, they felt an obligation in this regard. From time to time, they would even offer him a portion of their own scarce ration of bread so he might have something extra. They wanted to make this sacrifice on his behalf, they said, in order to express their faith in God and their gratitude to him for having sent a priest into their midst. Surely the hundredfold that Christ once promised to those who left father, mother, families, and country on his behalf was here handed out, not in any spectacular way but in the ordinary and simple actions of these generous believers through their small and continuous favors. For what they sacrificed, insignificant as it might seem, was actually a portion of all they had to survive on.

And the desire for survival was uppermost in the minds of everyone in the slave camps of Siberia. To live through it all and see freedom in the end was the secret hope everyone cherished. The instinct to live, to survive, especially for those who had a family or loved ones to return to, was the strongest motivation of every hour of every day. How conscious these men were of every day they lived. They counted it both as one day less in their sentence and yet one day less in their lives. No one wished, even for his bitterest enemy, the misfortune of dying in these camps away from everything a man held dear. And yet each day, they knew, was a step in the long slow march toward death.

It was to such men as these that I had been chosen, and was privileged, to bring the bread of life. "Unless you eat my flesh and drink my blood," Christ said to his disciples, "you shall not have life in you. He who eats my flesh and drinks my blood shall have life and have it more abundantly." These men, with simple and direct faith, grasped this truth and they believed in it. They could not explain it as a theologian might, but they accepted it and lived by it and were willing to make voluntary sacrifices even in a life of almost total deprivation, in order to receive this bread of life. Mass and the Blessed Sacrament were a source of great consolation to me; they were the source of my strength and joy and spiritual sustenance. But it was when I realized what the Holy Eucharist meant to these men, what sacrifices they were willing to make for it, that I felt animated, privileged, driven to make it possible for them to receive this bread of life as often as they wished. No danger, no risk, no retaliation could prevent my saying Mass each day for them. "As often as you do this, do it in memory of me." Life in the labor camps was Calvary for these men in many ways every day; there was nothing I would not do to offer the sacrifice of Calvary again for them each day in the Mass.

Chapter Fourteen

RETREATS

Life in the prison camps was a matter of endless and relentless routine. There were no diversions, no holidays, no vacations, no recreational activities for the prisoners. Work was the order of the day, every day, day after day, and one day followed the next with grinding and boring regularity, distinguished only from all other days by a change in the weather or the work to be done. There were days when the prisoner could take pride in what he had accomplished that day, even if it just meant taking satisfaction in the fact he had accomplished the quota of work set. A man needs something, some sense of accomplishment to maintain his sense of human dignity, of his value and worth as a person; even under the most stringent, most repetitious and boring routine, a man seeks for something to maintain his sense of dignity and of worth. Sometimes, in the harsh conditions of the camps, a man could get that satisfaction only from the knowledge that he as a person had survived the system one more day.

Days of labor in the long arctic twilight seemed endless, and followed one another in a seemingly endless stream. The work was hard, the conditions harsh, and meant to be so. Labor was the penalty a prisoner must pay for his transgressions against the state. He received only enough food to keep him alive, to make it just barely possible for him to continue work, and he worked each day until near exhaustion. Constantly hungry, always tired, the prisoners were thus kept in submission with little thought of revolt or of escape. For stretches of a month or more, prison authorities would keep us at work without a single day off. Signaled awake by an iron gong at 5 A.M., marched out to work for twelve to fourteen hours a day, marched back to camp for a meager meal of soup and kasha, always the same, then dropping exhausted on plank bunks in the barracks—such was the prisoner's routine as one day blurred monotonously into the next. Prison officials set the regime to keep the prisoners occupied to the maximum degree possible and so keep them in submission, but they also had to meet a quota of work set in Moscow and so gain the praise of higher authorities they sought after so scrupulously. The prisoners had no choice but to conform to the pattern set for them—the same daily routine year after year until it became habitual, a matter of boring routine without end or without hope, except that of ultimate survival.

The body might adjust to these conditions but the mind could not. Deprived of books, or even much chance for long conversations, each man was left to his own thoughts of the freedom he had lost, the life he led, and searched for some meaning to it all. To offset this, the prisoners were constantly bombarded with propaganda about the value of work, about their responsibility to share in building up the socialistic society they had damaged by their transgressions, about the need for even greater sacrifice, greater efforts, higher goals, and more work. Constant as they were, such exhortations made no impression at all on the prisoners. In its insistency, in its unsparing repetition, such propaganda seemed only another form of constant harassment. The prisoner recognized it for what it was, muttered about it, ignored it. He suffered it patiently for the most part, like everything else, longing only to survive to be free at last. And yet, the prisoners would tell you, even the end of the camps would not mean the end of the party line, or freedom from the pressure to work ever harder to build a new order, the new socialist world. There was no escaping it, nowhere where a man could go to live peacefully, to work and live normally, as he chose.

To survive in this situation, a man needed more than food or even intellectual sustenance, he needed spiritual strength. Accordingly, I organized a retreat movement in each of the camps as best I could. I began with the priests, who agreed to the idea eagerly. They, more than others, certainly realized the need for a strong spirit of faith, a deepened spiritual life. Many of them, too, felt this need especially because they were on the brink of discouragement and sometimes of despair. Priests were the object of special harassment in the camps, under constant surveillance by the authorities and always suspect. They were constantly called in for questioning, continually watched by informers, threatened, moved about from barracks to barracks to prevent any chance they might have of influencing other prisoners. Hampered in their work by this constant bullying, it was easy for them to get discouraged.

Worse yet were the larger doubts that assailed them when they were tired and discouraged. What could a handful of priests in the camp do, they would say, or what can individual priests dispersed all over the Soviet Union do to combat atheism and the propaganda directed against the Church and religion? What real chance had the Church to survive under such a system, where the people were constantly bombarded with reports that discredited religion as superstition, where the practice of religion was discouraged in so many ways and made difficult by so many subtle pressures, where a man could lose his job or the possibility of an education for his children because he was known to be a believer, or the children themselves were made fun of in school because their parents were believers, or were taught to despise the religious practices an older generation still clung to and talked about at home? How could a few priests, their numbers dwindling because seminaries were closed, ever hope to have much effect against the full power of the government and its propaganda? How could they do much good at all, when even those who still believed or wanted to believe in God were afraid to come to them or be seen with them for fear of reprisals at work, or the condemnation and hostility of friends or neighbors, or pressures brought indirectly to bear upon them and their families in so many ways? Humanly speaking, the task seemed hopeless and the future at best uncertain. It was all too easy to become discouraged, so the comfort of one another's company and the idea of retreats or days of recollection was eagerly accepted by them.

Many of our priests were older men, who tired easily. Unused to hard physical work and constantly bullied by prison authorities, they were frequently ill and required medical attention. Yet even the limited medical care available in the camp clinics was often denied them by the officials because they were priests. Their physical weakness and sickness only increased their sense of despondency and discouragement, their fear for the future of the Church as well as for themselves. Life in the camp deprived them of any of the external practices of religion they had known throughout their long priestly lives. Even at Mass, the external forms prescribed by the Church had to be largely discarded. Mass was said sitting down, sometimes walking about, sometimes half reclining, for the prescribed external rituals would only have called attention to what we were doing and brought the guards upon us quickly. It was hard for many of the older priests, try as they might, to practice a life of prayer and dedication without the support of the externals to which they had so long been accustomed.

In giving retreats to priests in the camps, I could take only one at a time. I followed the method of St. Ignatius, since it was what I knew best, recalling the meditations from memory and adapting them to the situations and circumstances of the camp. Points for each of the meditations were given in the morning at 6 A.M., before all the prisoners left the camp for work. At least half an hour was required to give the points properly, yet it was difficult to do, because at that time in the morning the whole camp was in turmoil. Prisoners poured out of the barracks, rushing in all directions—to the kitchen, storehouse, shoe repair shop, bakery, the warehouse, and infirmary. Everyone seemed anxious, concerned about something important, in a hurry, intent on seeing the doctor in order to get out of work, scrounging for extra food, on the lookout for an extra piece of clothing he might steal to guard him against the arctic cold, or on watch lest anything of his own be stolen. The camp guards, too, ran about like madmen from barracks to barracks, watching the prisoners and yelling at strays to return to their barracks and get ready for work. In the midst of all this excitement, I had to find a quiet place somewhere to be alone with my exercitant. In the evening, after work, it was much easier to get together and spend an hour or more with the prisoner priest to whom I was giving the retreat.

Retreats for priests, under these circumstances, generally lasted three days, occasionally five days, never much more than a week. Whenever possible, I tried to get other priests to help me in this work. Sometimes there were as many as three of us engaged in giving the individual retreats, so the others could have a choice of spiritual directors. For my part, I concentrated on the key meditations of the Exercises of St. Ignatius: the Principle and Foundation, the Kingdom, the Two Standards, and meditations on the passion of Christ. I felt it extremely important, given our circumstances, to strive to get them to realize again God's plan for man's salvation, to increase again their trust in him, to strengthen again their resolve to see his will in the events of every day—even such days as we were experiencing—and to strive to their utmost to fulfill that will with complete confidence in his providence and his power.

As priests, I emphasized, they had chosen to answer the call of Christ in a special way, even though it meant they might have to imitate in a special way his suffering to redeem the world. They had responded to his call to labor with him, to suffer with him, even to die with him, in order to bring others into the kingdom he came to establish. These prisoner-priests, especially, had been asked "to drink the cup that I must drink", as he once said to John and James. They had answered the call and made the promise, and Christ would be no less ready with his grace to see them through to the completion of the task to which he had called them.

It was easy to lose sight of this vision, to become discouraged, to feel helpless and useless as priests in the drab lives we led and the conditions under which we tried to work. But whoever has an easy life? The vision of the kingdom, the call of Christ to labor and suffer with him, has overtones of a great and noble crusade—yet we must each of us translate that vision and retain that spirit in the routine, humdrum events of every day, even days in a prison camp. It would be easy, we think to ourselves, to be constantly on fire with that vision if we could be a Francis Xavier or a Richard the Lion-Hearted, converting the Indies or scaling the walls of Jerusalem, sword in hand, caught up in the tumult of battle to win some great victory. We forget that Xavier, too, lived one day at a time, frustrated and perhaps discouraged, each twenty-four hours filled with as many defeats and frustrations as victories, each hour made up of sixty minutes of humdrum things and little people busy and concerned about many other things, day after day, week after week, month after month, year after year. As he went about trying to preach the gospel, how often must Xavier have wondered whether it would ever be possible to reach the millions of people around him? How often must he have felt discouraged at the individuals he met each day who failed to respond to his preaching? How often must he have despaired of the evil in the world around him, or felt helpless in the face of it?

I had little need to speak much of the power of evil to these prisoner-priests. It was tangible. It was all about us. That there was a force of evil loose in the world, doing battle for the minds of men, was as realistic as the barbed wire that fenced us in and the propaganda that bombarded us daily. So this was their battlefield, this was where Christ in his providence had seen fit to place them, this was where they must labor and suffer and perhaps die. Not in the Indies of the sixteenth century, not in the Holy Land of the twelfth century, not even in the equally humdrum and frequently frustrating routine of a parish life filled with days of people's problems and this world's concerns, but here in the seemingly hopeless conditions of a camp where men struggled simply to survive and took pride and comfort in having survived just one more day.

They had to convince themselves, these prisoner-priests, of the need to renew their faith in the belief that Christ's victory was the guarantee of their victory. The kingdom of God had to be worked out on earth, for that was the meaning of the Incarnation. It had to be worked out by men, by other Christs; it had to be worked out this day, each day, by constant effort and attention to just those persons and circumstances God presented to them that day. The "kingdom of God" had indeed been begun on earth with the coming of Christ, but the world had not visibly changed at his birth. Twelve Galilean fishermen had been instructed to tell the good news to the whole world—and how hopeless a task that must have seemed even to the boldest of them after Pentecost! Twenty centuries later, the kingdom of God was still a mustard

seed, and priests like themselves still faced the impossible task of
making men who had never believed, or who had yielded up
their beliefs under the pressure of daily life or a barrage of
propaganda, listen again to the good news of salvation and God's
love—and come to believe in him. That good news reached men
one at a time, by God's grace and according to his providence, not
in some great and visionary crusade or overnight through some
miraculous event. Each day, every day of our lives, God presents
to us the people and opportunities upon which he expects us to
act. He expects no more of us, but he will accept nothing less of
us; and we fail in our promise and commitment if we do not see in
the situations of every moment of every day his divine will.

That is how the kingdom of God has been spread from the
time of Christ's coming until now. It depends on the faith and
commitment of every man, but especially of the priest, every day
of his life. Every moment of every man's life is precious in God's
sight, and none must be wasted through doubt and discouragement.
The work of the kingdom, the work of laboring and suffering
with Christ, is no more spectacular for the most part than the
routine of daily living. Perhaps a priest experiences no spectacular
successes, at least as man measures successes, no miraculous
conversions, no enthusiastic displays of devotion, nothing dra-
matic at all. Yet he must come to believe, and be firmly convinced,
that Christ is the guarantor of his success. Christ has arranged for
him to be here, this day and among these people, in order that the
kingdom of God may be advanced in this place and among these
people. As a priest, he must be a witness in a special way to the
power of the kingdom to transform all things human, even the
tortured and twisted, the humdrum and the seemingly insignificant.
In fact, it is the unspectacular and the seemingly hopeless that are
the real challenge. For these things, too, must be transformed and
redeemed if Christ's victory is to be complete. The kingdom of
God will not be brought to fulfillment on earth by one great,
sword-swinging battle against the powers of darkness, but only
by each of us laboring and suffering day after day as Christ
labored and suffered, until all things at last have been transformed.
And this process of transformation continues to the end of time.

Only a deep renewal of faith in Christ, a renewed vision of how his kingdom is won in this world and a renewed sense of dedication to his will, could dispel the discouragement sometimes felt by these prisoner-priests, frightened because the power of evil and the seeming hopelessness of their cause dawned on them with all its clarity in the camps. The trials they were undergoing and had undergone were severe; perhaps, humanly speaking, too much for the priest to confront alone. Even the chance to talk with other priests in the camp and discuss the problems of religion, of the Church and the priesthood, proved insufficient to dispel all doubt and restore peace of mind. But the meditations of the retreat did seem to help these priests of little faith to renew and regain faith once again, to view the events around us in the light of the kingdom and the work of salvation in the world as it is. The retreat could not change things in the camp or make life better for the priest, but it had its effect on his soul nonetheless. It renewed his vision of his own life, and the lives of the men around him, in the light of God's providence and Christ's transforming power. It gave him new strength and new spirit to face the challenges of each day, under the cruelest of conditions, as opportunities that must not be missed for the building up of the kingdom of God.

With this in mind, too, we also tried to give retreats to the other prisoners whenever we could. It was not always easy, for even those who still kept their faith were not anxious at first to speak much at length about religion. Prisoners in general were slow to speak about such things anyhow, preoccupied as they were with the problem of sheer survival. Theirs was a simple faith and an even simpler morality. Lying, cheating, and stealing were a way of life in the prison camps; the prisoners justified it in their own minds as the only way to survive and as a way to cheat the system of its absolute domination over their lives. There were few tender consciences in the camps about such matters. A man did what he had to do to survive at all costs. They might mention such things in confession because they had learned to, but it was hard for them to feel any compunction. Sometimes it was almost as if they were asking God's approval of these practices rather than his forgiveness or pardon. They wanted to be "straight" with God, but they also had to survive in this cruel and unjust system—and they hoped he would understand.

That was what really surprised us about these men: the simplicity and directness of their belief in God and the tenacity of their faith and trust in him. Even the consciousness of their sins and failings expressed in confession served only, it seemed, to strengthen this faith. If God had preserved him this far, a prisoner would tell you, if he had not rejected him with all his transgressions but had kept him alive until now, then surely he would not abandon him. That was the source of their confidence and trust in him. God could be counted on when man could not, he would help even if friends and all else failed. He had proved that up to now. God was a prisoner's ultimate hope of survival, his last resort. No matter what a man had done, how he had failed God or his fellowman, God had not yet abandoned him and could be counted on to sustain him again tomorrow.

Retreats for these prisoners were more of a mission, really. We tried to build on the confidence and trust in God that they already clung to and counted on, to encourage them to become still closer to God through the sacraments, through more frequent confession and Communion. And we tried, moreover, to help them understand that their lives were not lost or wasted, but still precious in God's sight. That was why he had not, and would not, abandon them. Over and over again we spoke of God's providence, though, as more than just his care and concern for them, that care and concern they already felt so strongly. We tried to help them see that their lives, too, had meaning; that their work and their sufferings had a value each day; that there could still be dignity in what they did in God's eyes, if not in men's. So we taught them to say the Morning Offering—to dedicate to God all the prayers, works and sufferings of each day in conformity to his will—as a means of winning grace for others, especially for their families and friends.

In that way, no matter how harsh the conditions in the camps might be, how cruel and useless the work might seem, it took on new meaning and added value. It was something of which a man could be proud each day, because it was his to offer back to God. Each day of labor and hardship, like the grains of wheat ground up to make the host at Mass, could be consecrated to God and be transformed into something of great value in God's sight; it was a sacrifice each man could offer back to God throughout the long, hard days. The grinding routine of daily labor, even here in Siberia, could have a meaning, did have a value, even as the lives of all men everywhere—no matter how dull or routine or insignificant they might seem to the eyes of men—have a value and a meaning in God's providence.

Chapter Fifteen

THE FEAR OF DEATH

Facing a firing squad is a pretty good test, I guess, of your theology of death. I didn't exactly pass the test with flying colors. Perhaps it all just happened too quickly, without any warning. There had been a revolt of the prisoners at Camp 5 in Norilsk, and when troops were called in to put down the revolt they divided the prisoners up into small groups and marched them off. I was rounded up in a group of thirty, one of the first groups herded out of the camp and led down to a sandpit about a mile away. We had no idea what disciplinary measures would be taken against us, but we never for a moment thought we would see the soldiers line up five yards in front of us with rifles ready, waiting only for the command to shoot. The command was given, the rifles raised, cocked on another command, and leveled at our heads. For a moment, as if in a dream, none of us really understood what was happening. Then the realization that we were actually looking into gun barrels awaiting only the command to fire came crashing into my consciousness with a force that stopped everything. My stomach turned once and went numb; my heart stopped; I'm sure I forgot to breathe; I couldn't move a muscle in my body; my mind went blank.

The first thought I actually remember thinking was a question: "Is this the end, Lord?" I know I started the act of contrition, but I remember the sensation of realizing that another part of me could not understand the words I was mumbling. The other part of me focused on the fact that in a fraction of a second I would stand before God, dumbfounded and unprepared, unable in the suddenness of my confusion and total terror to feel sorry for my sins, numbed into absolute inactivity, unable so much as to elicit a simple act of faith in the God I had learned to trust implicitly in every action of every day, let alone think with anticipation of meeting him face to face at last. I can still remember vividly my awareness of the moment, and the second fear that gripped me, when I realized I was incapable of performing any Christian act to redeem myself, paralyzed and terrified and yet conscious of what I should be doing—indeed was trying to do by rotely reciting the act of contrition without comprehension or meaning—in the last moment of life left to me before the veil parted and I would stand before God.

I have no idea how long that one moment lasted. Suddenly there was a shot in the distance, shouts, and a group of officers dashed out to stop our execution. All I know is that when the moment passed, my heart was pounding, every nerve and muscle shaking, my knees weak and trembling, my mind once again able to follow the sequence of events in a coherent way. When we were finally marched off again, I tried to figure out what had happened to me.

Often enough, during the years of prison, of interrogations, of life in the camps, I had lived with the thought of death. On more than one occasion, I had been told I would be shot, and I knew those threats were truly meant. I had seen men die around me of starvation or illness or sometimes just out of a lack of wanting to live any longer. I had faced death in my mind time and time again, had helped others in their final moments, had lived with the talk and presence of death. I had thought about it and reflected on it, had no fear of it, sometimes looked forward to it. What was there, then, about this moment that so terrified me, so completely unstrung me and made me incapable of functioning, of praying, even of thinking? Was it just the suddenness, the surprise, that had betrayed me?

That had to be part of it. Then, too, there was the physical fear. Everyone, sometime in his life, has experienced the effects of a sudden fright, a bad scare—a close call in an accident, perhaps, or an unexpected fall, maybe just a sudden, loud, strange noise. Animal instinct takes over at such moments; the mind goes blank, the body reacts: muscles tense, the heart quickens, the stomach tightens, nerves tingle. And when the moment passes, if it passes without physical contact or bodily harm, a reaction sets in as the body grows limp. Those are simply the physical signs of fear, and it is not surprising that the body should fear injury or even death. I cannot be sure—perhaps I will never know for certain until the moment of death approaches again—but I suspect that most of my panic before the firing squad in that sandpit outside Norilsk was due to such animal instinct in the face of a sudden and totally unexpected physical danger.

For the thought of death itself does not terrify me, had not terrified me all through the war, or prison, or the prison camps. Death must come to all men at the end of this earthly life, but it is not therefore evil. If the good news of Christianity is anything, it is this: that death has no hidden terror, has no mystery, is not something man must fear. It is not the end of life, of the soul, of the person. Christ's death on Calvary was not in itself the central act of salvation, but his death *and* resurrection; it was the resurrection that completed his victory over sin and death, the heritage of man's original sin that made a Redeemer and redemption necessary. This was the "good news" of salvation, meant to remove mankind's last doubts, last fears, about the nature of death. For the resurrection was a fact, a fact as certain and as sure as death itself, and it meant that death held no victory over men, that life beyond death is a certainty and not just a human hope or fable. This was the fact that made new men of his once fearful disciples, this was the "good news" they preached. The little sermons recorded in the Acts of the Apostles center on this theme: God has raised Christ up from the dead, he has risen, and of that fact we are witnesses.

From the fall of Adam, God had promised a Redeemer. From the day death came into the world, God has promised a conqueror of death. And the good news to be preached throughout the world was that the Redeemer had come, death had been conquered! This is the joy of Easter, this is the peace it brings. "O foolish and slow of heart to believe," he said to the two disciples on their way to Emmaus, "ought not the Christ to have suffered these things, and so entered into his glory?" The victory of God's "annointed one", the Messiah, was to be over the "kingdom" of death and of sin, but how could he triumph unless he first suffered death and then broke its chains? Easter was the victory, Easter was the "good news" the apostles were sent to preach to the ends of the earth. And the joy of Easter is the joy of that good news, while the peace of Easter is the peace that comes from knowing that the thing men had feared most—the end of life, annihilation, death—really holds no fear at all.

That is not a Christian fable; it is a fact, and the proof of it is the resurrection. "If Christ be not risen," said St. Paul to his Christians, "then your faith is in vain." You cannot be a Christian and doubt that fact. Christ's coming upon earth, his taking on of human flesh, had no purpose if it was not to die and then to triumph over death. He was not just a religious leader, a great teacher of ethics or morals, he was the Promised One, the Savior, the Messiah. His death and resurrection are the central facts not just of Christianity but of all human history. Men lived in expectation of his coming and his victory over death, until at last he came; since then, the "good news" of his victory over death has been proclaimed everywhere and has sustained in peace and joy those who have believed.

Perhaps nowhere on earth is the contrast between those who believe and those who do not believe more striking than it is in the Soviet Union. Death is very nearly a taboo subject in the communist milieu. In an ideology of atheistic materialism, death is obviously the end of everything for a man. It is a special tragedy for the young, who are cut off from life just as they are beginning to live: it is tragic for those in middle age, who have reached the peak of their powers; for the old, who have lived a full life, it may come as a release but it is no less an end to life and therefore tragic. A man might survive in the memory of his loved ones, a famous man's reputation might keep his name alive somewhat longer than most, but for the rest death meant not only the end of *this* life but of all existence. A dedicated communist could work to build a better society for his heirs, for those who came after him, but he himself could not survive. Men are exhorted to take pride in their work, to build a better tomorrow for all mankind, but this can be their only hope. Marx and Lenin laid down the foundation of the doctrine: today's communists should consider it a privilege and an honor to be the pioneers of a new social order, a grandiose revolutionary tide sweeping on to worldwide communism. Life therefore requires a total sacrifice of self to the great cause of building communism, and no thought of death should be allowed to detract from this purpose. As a result, practical measures were taken in the Soviet Union to avoid mentioning anything about death.

When death occurs, of course, it affects the immediate family and relatives and friends as well. If a party functionary or some distinguished worker dies, there will be some display and eulogies of his achievements. A bouquet or two of flowers, with slogans attached, mark the grave as a sign of distinction and honor. Perhaps a band accompanies the funeral cortege, and party colleagues pay their last respects by attending or speaking at the graveside. The ordinary citizen, however, dies and is buried nearly unnoticed.

Funerals generally take place after work, so that those who wish to attend may do so; work cannot be interrupted because of someone's burial. The ordinary coffin consists of a few planks held together in the form of a trough, covered around with a cloth like gauze dyed red. That is all. The cost of such a coffin is at most five rubles. The truck used to transport the coffin to the cemetery is loaned free of charge by the enterprise where the comrade worked, and it, too, is available only in the hours after work—when the factory five-year plan will not be interrupted by the use of a truck for some other purpose such as a funeral. That the truck had spent the day hauling gravel, men, dirt, and other materials mattered little to the driver or the people who would use it after hours as a hearse. A few strokes of a broom sufficed to clean the dirt from the platform; the tailboards would be lowered, and the truck would be ready for the funeral.

No pomp accompanied the funeral procession. A small group of the immediate family, together with a few friends, followed the slowly moving truck in silence and deep sorrow. Side streets were assigned to be used for funerals, which must skirt busy intersections or main thoroughfares, so that other citizens would not be unnecessarily distracted or affected by the sight of a funeral procession. The less people witness such sad scenes, said officials, the better. For communism lays stress on the joys of life, on man's progress, not on sorrow and despair. And yet the passersby along the line of march were touched. Many stopped and stood with heads uncovered to show their sympathy for the dead and for the grieving family. Others actually knelt on the sidewalk and made the sign of the cross, remaining in that posture until the procession passed, for the thought of death touches human nature much too closely.

There has always been a strain of mysticism in Russia on this subject, as the writings of Dostoyevsky, Tolstoy, and other great Russian writers clearly show. Even among non-believers, the strain of mysticism remains to this day. It is quite common, especially in the towns and villages, for the anniversaries of the death of loved ones to be strictly observed. On the day of the anniversary, family and friends visit the grave at the cemetery and decorate it again with flowers. Christians will also place upon the grave blessed medals or icons, and try if possible to have the grave blessed again by a priest on the day of the anniversary. Soviet law, however, now forbids priests to bless graves at the cemetery, so the people ask that the office of the dead be sung at the church for the dear one whose anniversary they celebrate.

At home, relatives and friends are invited to a meal especially prepared for the occasion. Rolls of all kinds are baked, stuffed with meat or fish or cheese or vegetables such as cabbage, carrots, and onions. Big pancakes are served with sour cream, butter, or some jam if it can be gotten. Then a big bowl of cooked rice with raisins and honey is placed in the center of the table at the end of the meal. Each guest takes a spoonful of the honeyed rice as he mentions the name of the deceased person whose anniversary is being celebrated, expressing at the same time his sympathy for the family and recalling the good deeds of the loved one. It is a sort of religious ceremony, reliving in spirit the presence of the departed in the company of family, friends, and relatives. Tears are shed, the day of burial is relived in words and memories; in this way a solidarity of the living with the dead is upheld, paying tribute in the fullest manner possible to those who have died.

The Tuesday after the Sunday after Easter (Low Sunday) is a special day for the commemoration of the dead. Crowds flock to the cemeteries, bearing food and flowers, almost as if for a picnic. The graves are cleaned and decorated and then the family sits down to a meal at the graveside. Passersby are invited to join the meal or to drink a toast. On that day, too, Christians used to ask the priest to sing a special requiem service, called the Panikhida, at the graveside. There were times, during my later years in Norilsk, when I was kept busy from early morning to late at night going from grave to grave to sing these services for families. This, too, is now forbidden and indeed the Komsomol organizations and the League of Militant Atheists crusade constantly in the press to have these annual observances banned, on the grounds that they lead to public disorder and drunkenness. But the observances continue, and it is a rare sight to witness how, on that day, everyone comes to the cemetery to pay homage to the dead. Communists as well as non-communists come to show their respects, not only to their own departed relatives but to those of friends and neighbors as well, sharing with them their memories and feelings of grief, finding in all this some consolation and some bond of union with them in expressions of tender and moving love.

One could sense in all this, among these simple ordinary people, communists and non-communists alike, a desire somehow to preserve a link with those who had died, to keep their memories alive at least, to cling to some small hope that death was not the end of man's existence. It was an instinct, deep in the Russian character and tradition, that all the learned assertions of the would-be experts on the question of death in the press, on radio, and on TV, could not shake. The people sensed deeply what life meant to them, and they could not bring themselves to believe that death was the end of all. The family at least must remember.

I think, for example, of the dear old *babushka* (grandmother) of the family with whom I lived for six years in Abakan before my final return to the United States. She loved to talk with me because I would listen. Somewhat forgetful, she would tell me the experiences of her seventy-six years over and over each day. She often talked of her departed husband: how she had visited him in prison, how he suffered being sick, how she did everything she could for him till the very day of his death. Her greatest sorrow came from the fact that her husband had died in prison, away from home and family. She considered that a great tragedy, not just for him but for the family. She often told me how sorry she felt for me, alone in the Soviet Union without a family, and told me how she prayed I might someday return to the United States and die in my own country with my family and relatives close by. She thought that dying in a strange country would be a terrible thing, to die without a loved one at your bedside the greatest tragedy.

The fear of death, the fact of death, affects all men; and yet the strain of mysticism about death that runs so deep in Russian literature and folk customs seems to heighten the poignancy of this universal phenomenon even more. It is to these fears that the "good news" of Christianity speaks. I found it especially among the simple people, the good people, for whom the desire or the expectation of an afterlife was not a fantasy or an illusion, as they so often heard it described by communist propagandists. It was more than a belief; it was something real, something that all the assertions of the learned materialists, the proofs of science, and classroom demonstrations could not shake. Death to them was not an end, but a beginning, a passage into eternal life. They took joy in the fact that they would one day be together with their loved ones again, and sometimes longed to be free of the sorrows of this life and to be at peace at last with God forever.

Salvation, these simple people would say, is not measured in terms of how well we make out in what we do here on earth; it depends ultimately on our belief in God and our abandonment in him. In failure or in success, in health or sickness, in sorrow or joy, man must turn to God, must trust in God, believing in him more each day, loving him more each day, in preparation for a future life with him. There was something beautiful in their simplicity, something that all the theologians and books of theology could not match in their approach to death. That I should find it in the Soviet Union startled me at first. It taught me much. And coupled with my own experience, it made me think, and think deeply, about the meaning of death for a Christian.

What is there to fear in death? It means no more and no less than the end of our testing period here on earth; it is a return, a going home, to the God and Father who first created us. It is not the end of life; the fact of the resurrection proves that beyond a doubt. There is sorrow in our separation from family and friends, no doubt, the human sorrow of which no one need feel ashamed. And yet, as St. Paul says, we Christians do not grieve as ones who have no hope; we believe in the resurrection, as we say in our profession of faith, the Creed, and in the life of the world to come. Death is not a tragedy in our belief, but only an ordained passage from this life to the next.

Death may be feared by those who do not believe, who have no hope. It may be feared by those whose faith in Christ and the resurrection is weak, or those who fear to meet God face to face because of what they have done or how they have lived in this period of testing we call life on earth. Men may legitimately worry, too, about those they leave behind; Christians have always prayed to be delivered from "a sudden and unprovided death". But death itself is not a thing we fear. It is a homecoming, the return of the prodigal son, perhaps, to the welcoming arms of a loving father. We expect it, as all men must, but we expect it in confidence and even joy, buoyed up by our faith in Christ and his victory over death.

Christ has risen, and our faith is not in vain. The resurrection is a fact, a fact of recorded human history and of what the theologians call "salvation history". So death for us is not an enemy, a thing to be dreaded, a word we prefer not to think about or play down as do the communists. We think and speak about it not as an end to everything but as the end of our probation. We can anticipate it daily, and even eagerly, because of our faith. We can learn to yearn for it, prepare ourselves for it, and embrace it gladly, in joy and in peace, when at last we are called home to our heavenly inheritance. This we believe; this essentially is what it means to be a Christian—one who believes in Christ, the promised Redeemer and victor over sin and death.

Chapter Sixteen

FREEDOM

Many a time, during the years I was in prison or the labor camps of Siberia, officials and interrogators told me I would never again go free in the Soviet Union. Sometimes they said it sarcastically, sometimes threateningly, sometimes merely matter-of-factly. When I was called in for interrogations in the prison camp, as all priests were on a regular basis, it was almost a certainty that sometime in the conversation a camp official would assure me I would never see freedom again. Of course they knew and I knew that my term was officially fifteen years, but that fact was shrugged off almost as a sort of legal fiction; besides, there were so many technical violations and minor infractions of the camp rules going on at all times that officials could always find some excuse to tack on an added term if they wanted. They were in charge, their word was law, and the prisoner had no recourse to the courts or much hope of appealing to higher authority in such a case. Even my fellow prisoners, in casual conversation, nearly always took it for granted I would never see the end of my term or the outside of prison-camp barbed wire. They would wag their heads sympathetically and shrug their shoulders, but they accepted it as just another fact of the systematic injustice we had to endure, regrettable but a foregone conclusion. After a while, even I came to believe it and accept it as a fact of life.

One spring morning, however, in the prison camp of Kayerkhan, I was called to the camp office before work and told I would be liberated in ten days. Checking my records, the camp officials had found that according to some new regulations I was entitled to three months off my term; I actually served, therefore, only fourteen years and nine months of my fifteen-year sentence. So, in the next few evenings after work, I began a round of medical examinations and the red tape of paper work that preceded a prisoner's release. The night before I was actually to be released, I didn't sleep a wink; I simply couldn't believe that after fifteen years I would really be free again. About nine o'clock the next morning the foreman called me from the barracks and took me to the KGB (the internal security police) office, where I sat for about two hours signing documents and filling out forms. I kept expecting some trouble or possibly another interrogation, but the men on duty went about it all quite routinely, paying no more attention to me than they would to any other prisoner being set free. Finally, everything was in order and one of the officials explained in great detail my new status.

Those who leave the prison camps are not fully free; instead of the passport issued to and carried by all Soviet citizens, ex-prisoners get a so-called "document of liberation," which is a certificate stating that you have completed your sentence. Even then, a distinction is made. A prisoner may either be fully liberated and rehabilitated, or only partially, as in my case. As a convicted spy, I got what is known as a restricted certificate or *polozenie pasporta*. With it, I was restricted as to where I could live and where I could work. I wasn't allowed, for example, to live in any "regime city", i.e., the big cities like Leningrad, Moscow, Kiev, Vladivostok, Tashkent, or in any of the border cities from which, presumably, I might try to leave the country. I could visit such places for periods not to exceed three days, with the express permission of the police and the government. And, with a *polozenie pasporta,* one of the first things I had to do in any city was report to the police and register my presence there.

After the officials had explained all this to me, and checked out my camp documents for what seemed the hundredth time, they told me to go directly to Norilsk when I left the camp and report to the police there. The police, they said, would give me a formal set of identity papers so I would be able to settle down in the city as a free citizen. By noon of an April day in Siberia, all the paper shuffling and explanations were over, and I walked out the main gate of the camp for the last time. Automatically, after I had gone about fifteen paces beyond the gate, I stopped and waited for the guards, as we prisoners did every morning on the way to work. The guards at the gate watched me and laughed—nine out of ten liberated prisoners made the same mistake out of force of habit.

I was so self-conscious, I didn't know how to walk like a free man. My arms, dangling at my sides rather than folded behind my back, felt strange. I turned to take a last, long look at the camp, almost as if I'd have to tear myself away, and then put my hands in my pockets and walked toward the town of Kayerkhan. There was a train at the station. I climbed on board and no one challenged me or paid the slightest attention to me. I couldn't believe it. The conductor, a woman, collected my fare. I kept expecting her to ask me questions or to raise a difficulty of some sort. She just smiled politely. I sat down in the seat looking out the window, almost in tears—a free man, treated like a free man. I kept waiting for something to happen, for somebody to shout or something to stop the train or someone to point at me. Yet nothing happened. The train began to move, and I was free at last.

I guess perhaps you have to be deprived of freedom in order truly to realize how precious a gift it is. Certainly one of the greatest torments to those in prison or in the prison camps was the knowledge and remembrance of what it had once meant to be free. The strict regime of the prisons and the camps only aggravated this feeling, for there everything was fixed; not only was there confinement behind bars or barbed wire, but the minutest details of the daily order were fixed and inflexible. The prisoner made no decisions for himself. There was a fixed time to rise, a fixed time to report for work, a fixed time for recreation or exercise, a fixed time to retire at night. There were fixed times, too, for the meager meals, and if a man missed them for any reason, he simply went hungry. But worse than all these physical restrictions was the awful realization, beaten into a man by bitter experience and constantly repeated by officials, that a prisoner was a person without rights and to be treated as such. He became, in truth, a thing rather than an individual, with no respect for his dignity or his person or even for his existence as a human being.

He was a number, and most often addressed by the guards and officials simply by his prison number.

Some men were simply shattered by this realization. Some took refuge in thoughts only of the past, trying to blot out the awful realities of the present and in that way find an escape from the grim life of the camps. Some fell into fits of depression that gradually grew more intense under the pressures of camp life; some of them simply gave up even the thought of hope and the will to go on. Few such people ever survived. It was only those who accepted the bitter loss of freedom, galling as it was, and resolved to follow their instincts for survival who managed at last to walk out of the camps again. They banded together and formed friendships, almost like fraternity brothers, because instinct told them that a man alone ran the risk of losing out in the long run. Being with others, constantly communicating with them, gave a man some assurance. He had lost everything, his life was always exposed to the danger of sickness or a physical disability, even of death, and yet he was not alone. Someone in the barracks cared—even if he could not do much to help but could only console. Even this much, however, served to restore to some degree a prisoner's sense of human dignity, his sense of worth as a person. He in turn could feel sympathy with his friend's loss of freedom and uncertain future, could share his hope of survival, his memories of the past, his thoughts of the future.

The body can be confined, but nothing can destroy the deepest freedom in man, the freedom of the soul, and the freedom of mind and will. These are the highest and noblest faculties in man, they are what make him the sort of man he is, and they cannot be constrained. Even in prison a man retains his free will, his freedom of choice. Even in prison, a man can choose to do good or evil, to fight for survival or to despair, to serve God and others or to turn inward and selfish. Free will remains and so freedom remains, for freedom is simply defined as the state of being free, not coerced by necessity or fate or circumstances in one's choices or actions.

That freedom is absolute, and yet freedom itself is not an absolute as many today would have us believe. Young people, too, often yearn for freedom and independence as if these were somehow absolutes. They speak of freedom as of a good in itself, as if it existed in some ideal order, unfettered by obligations and duty. This drive for independence and freedom on the part of the young is a natural thing, a part of the process of growing up, of becoming mature individuals, of cutting the apron strings and preparing for adult life. Yet parents fail in their duty to their children if they let this tendency go unchecked, unrestrained, and do not insist that children exercise their freedom in the context of duties and obligations at home and in school, to parents and family, to friends and to those in authority. For the adult world that a child so ardently desires to attain, that he looks forward to so eagerly and impatiently, is also a world in which freedom is greatly modified by circumstances, by concrete obligations and limitations, and it is only in this real world of daily life that human freedom, such as it is, exists, and not in some ideal order.

In a democratic society, freedom quite often suffers from its abuse by others rather than any legal restraints to its exercise, yet suffer it does. Sometimes it happens, it seems, because the laws or those who enforce them are too permissive and fail to punish adequately those who transgress the rights of others. In a totalitarian state, on the other hand, freedom suffers from lack of exercise, for the laws are stringent, the penalties severe, and authorities themselves curtail the rights of citizens. The fact is that the causes which limit the freedom of man in the concrete and real world we live in are many, whether it be freedom of speech or of conscience, whether it be civil or social or religious or personal freedom. No matter under what aspects you consider the notion of freedom, you will always find difficulties in this life that cannot be solved and so render to each man the full freedom he desires.

I sat in the train headed for Norilsk, exhilarated by my new freedom, and yet thinking such thoughts. What did it mean for me to be free, for any man to be free? I was out of the prison camps and free from the rigorous daily order, free to order my own life, free to make each day's decisions for myself. In that sense I was free, yet I was not free of all restrictions. There were certain restrictions on me especially as an ex-prisoner, there would always be special restrictions on me as long as I carried the *polozenie pasporta.* Yet these restrictions differed only in detail from the restrictions that bind every man in every society: the rules and observances, laws and customs, even the "accepted" traditions of family, church, society, or culture. No man's freedom is absolute.

Ultimately, the only absolute freedom we have resides in a man's free will. And that freedom was given us by our Creator, essentially, so that we might freely choose to love and serve him. All other creatures serve him out of exigency; by their very being and existence they witness to his power and his love, or reflect his glory and beauty in some way. Only to man and the angels has he given the power of freely choosing to love and serve him. He has made us a little less than the angels, has given us intellect and free will—and that is the hallmark of man, at once his crowning glory, his most precious gift, his most terrifying responsibility. Only man can freely choose not to serve his Creator.

It is in choosing to serve God, to do his will, that man achieves his highest and fullest freedom. It may seem paradoxical to say that our highest and fullest freedom comes when we follow to the least detail the will of another, but it is true nonetheless when that other is God. I could testify from my own experiences, especially from my darkest hours in Lubianka, that the greatest sense of freedom, along with peace of soul and an abiding sense of security, comes when a man totally abandons his own will in order to follow the will of God. Never again could I doubt that the greatest assurance I could have in my life came from knowingly and willingly following God's will as manifested to me. I knew only too well how shallow and unsafe it was for me to follow my own will, my own inclinations and desires, unless they were in conformity to his. I realized then, and I felt it more deeply each day, that true freedom meant nothing else than letting God operate within my soul without interference, giving preference to God's will as manifested in the promptings, inspirations, and other means he chose to communicate, rather than in acting on my own initiatives.

For those who do not believe in God, I suppose, such thoughts will seem sheer nonsense or unexplainable stupidity. For me, however, there could be no doubt: the fullest freedom I had ever known, the greatest sense of security, came from abandoning my will to do only the will of God. What was there to fear so long as I did his will? Not death. Not failure, except the failure to do his will. "For if God is with us, who can stand against us?" Choosing to do his will and experiencing the spiritual freedom that followed was my greatest joy and the source of tremendous interior strength. For to know that he directed me in all my actions, that he sustained me with his grace, gave me a sense of peace and courage beyond description. Even in moments of human discouragement, the consciousness that I was fulfilling God's will in all that happened to me would serve to dispel all doubt and desolation. Whatever the trials of the moment, whatever the hardships or sufferings, more important than all these was the knowledge that they had been sent by God and served his divine providence. I could not always fathom the depths of his providence or pretend to understand his wisdom, but I was secure in the knowledge that by abandoning myself to his will I was doing as perfectly as I could his will for me.

Spiritual freedom of this sort, as I knew from bitter experience, is not something that can be attained overnight or ever possessed in its final form. Every new day, every new hour of every day, every new circumstance and situation, every new act is a new opportunity to exercise and grow in this freedom. What is required for growth is an attitude of acceptance and openness to the will of God, rather than some planned approach or calculated method. Even ascetical practices such as penances, fasting, or mortifications can be hindrances rather than helps if they are self-imposed. Striving instead to eliminate all self-will, to accept God's will revealed in the circumstances of daily life, is the surest way to achieve growth in conformity to the will of God. It will provide more than enough virtue to be practiced, suffering to be sustained, pain to be borne; more importantly still, it will make us fit instruments to achieve his designs, not only for our own salvation but for others as well. The service of God must take preference over all else.

A spirituality based on complete trust in God, therefore, is the surest guarantee of peace of soul and freedom of spirit. In it the soul must learn to act not on its own initiative, but in response to whatever demands are imposed by God in the concrete instances of each day. Its attention must always be centered precisely and primarily on God's will as revealed and manifested in the people, places, and things he sets before us, rather than on the means required to fulfill it. Then no matter what these means demand— suffering, risk, loneliness, or physical hardships such as hunger or sickness—the consciousness of fulfilling God's will in accepting them makes the sacrifice easy, the burden light. There is no other reason to accept sacrifice or mortification; indeed to seek them for any other motive than conformity to the will of God is the sign of some spiritual distortion. But accepting whatever comes or happens as the will of God, no matter what it costs spiritually, psychologically, or physically, is the surest and quickest way to a freedom of soul and spirit that surpasses all understanding and explanation.

The train ride from Kayerkhan to Norilsk was not such a long one. It brought to mind again, however, that first long train ride into Russia from Lvov, when I had been so sure that I was doing the will of God. That had truly been my reason for coming, but how imperfectly I had understood it then. How much I had learned in the meantime, how often I had failed, how painful the lessons had been. And now I was going at last, as a free man, to begin again what I had dreamed of doing then: serving the people of the Soviet Union as a priest insofar as I was able, helping them attain eternal salvation by serving and loving God. Physically, I might not be as free to do as much as I might wish; I had to register with the police as soon as I reached Norilsk, and I would surely be kept under surveillance. But spiritually I had never felt freer, or more secure in the conviction that God watched over me always and directed me along the paths marked out by his divine providence.

Chapter Seventeen

THE KINGDOM OF GOD

The first thing I did when I reached Norilsk was look for a Ukrainian priest, Father Viktor, who had been in one of the camps with me and released four months earlier. I knew that he, too, had been given a restricted passport and sent to Norilsk. After asking around, I finally found him in a shanty-town out on the edge of the city. A random jumble of shanties, huts, and shacks (called *boloks*) that had once housed a large group of Chinese "volunteer" workers in Siberia, it was still called "Shanghai Town" by the people of Norilsk. Its huts and shacks were made of old boards and packing crates, built one onto the other like a series of dominoes. The walls were usually double, made of odds and ends of thin scrap lumber, then filled with ashes for insulation. Some of the better ones were covered with tar paper or clay or plaster on the outside. I found Father Viktor living in one of these *boloks* together with another priest, Father Neron, who had also been an inmate in the prison mining camp of Kayerkhan I had just left, but he had been liberated before I was sent there.

In this little *bolok*, perhaps ten by ten feet square, they had two beds separated by an altar; for this little room, in fact, served as their chapel too. They were so cramped and crowded that I asked Father Viktor if he knew of some family in the neighborhood with whom I could stay. But he and Neron wouldn't hear of it. They were delighted to see me and insisted that I stay with them. They cooked me a dinner on the little electric stove that served both for cooking and for heating the *bolok*. Then we talked for hours. That night we placed three chairs in a line, in the little space between the two beds in front of the altar, and I slept there, using my padded prison coat and pants—the only clothes I had to my name—as mattress, blanket, and pillow. As soon as we got up in the morning, we cleared out the beds and prepared to celebrate Mass.

By six-thirty, there were ten or twelve people in that little room for Mass. On Sundays, the people jammed not only this room but the corridor beyond the open door as well. To accommodate the growing crowd, Viktor and Neron said two Masses every Sunday and preached a sermon at each, and there might be sixty or more people at every Mass. For this ramshackle *bolok* was, in effect, their "parish" church. On most evenings, too, there was generally a congregation of some sort: for confessions, or baptisms, or a wedding, or a Panikhida, the very beautiful Russian memorial service chanted for the dead.

The crowds were so great, in fact, that I soon began taking a valise full of Mass equipment provided by Viktor every Sunday morning to another part of the city—to an old prison camp, actually—to say Mass for another "parish" of Poles, in one of the old camp barracks now used for city housing. Before Mass, I'd hear confessions; then, after Mass, I'd have baptisms and weddings, in ever increasing numbers as the people found out I was available every Sunday. I registered with the police as I had been instructed to do, then got a job, and was finally able to get a little *bolok* of my own. There, too, I said Mass every day for a constantly growing number of people, but I continued to say Mass on Sunday for my Polish "parish" out in the old camp barracks.

I was constantly under surveillance by the police, of course, and so were my parishioners. Occasionally I would be called in for questioning and warned against "agitating" of the people. I knew that some of them were also interrogated by the police, or harassed by union officials or supervisors where they worked, about practicing religion so openly. But I was amazed and consoled by the constancy of their faith and their courage in the face of these minor persecutions, so I was determined to continue to help them as long as I could. Even if it meant being arrested again, or sent back to prison or the camps, I was willing to run that risk in order to serve as a priest for these courageous Christians.

Frankly, I often marveled at the way these people had clung to the faith in this professedly atheistic country. Atheism was taught and preached everywhere, in the newspapers, on radio and television, in the schools, and in books and periodicals of all sorts. The Soviet Constitution, of course, guarantees every citizen the right to practice religion, but it forbids any formal preaching or teaching about religion. In fact, the law has been interpreted to mean that children under eighteen years of age are not allowed to attend church, even in the company of their parents, and priests are forbidden to give religious instructions to youth. The same article of the constitution that guarantees freedom to practice religion but not to preach it also guarantees the freedom of atheistic propaganda. And that guarantee was exercised to the full by the state in every conceivable way. Everyone, from the youngest child to the oldest grandparent, was constantly exposed and subjected to the influence of such propaganda. The effect of all this upon once Holy Russia has been to change the entire social life of the country, the manner of thinking and behavior of the average citizen. And yet, for all that, it has not affected the faith of millions of believers.

Even as atheism exerts its influence everywhere in the country, so do the Orthodox Church and the other religious sects, despite the overwhelming odds against them and the great difficulty under which they labor. The churches are few and far between. No Bibles or religious literature can be bought or published. No Church periodicals or religious papers or pamphlets were available to the people. At some of the Orthodox monasteries, however, small icons, prayer beads, candles, and holy cards with a short prayer printed on the back are still available, and the people cherish and treasure them. The churches hold services on Sunday or Saturday evening. To hold services on other days, such as major Church feasts, the priest stationed at the church must depend on the good offices of a committee which arranges for all services and administers the church affairs.

These church committees are directly responsible to the government. Their job is to oversee everything, even the sermons—which must be strictly confined to religious topics, usually short, and carefully selected to avoid any allusions to politics or criticism of the government, party, or system. The Orthodox Church, which is still the "official" religion of Russia, receives some government subsidies for the maintenance of historic Church structures, as well as a small salary for the priest which is doled out by the church committee. It is paradoxical, to be sure, that the atheistic government of the Soviet Union has a special Ministry of Cults (Religious Affairs) that even provides funds for church affairs; but this same ministry also serves as an organ of tight control over the churches and all their affairs. The organized Orthodox Church and its hierarchy, therefore, can do little to counteract the strong influence of the government which works against the purity of its spiritual structure.

The people were well aware of what was going on. Sometimes they grumbled about the fact that the clergy and bishops didn't react to such government interference in church affairs. Few could or did, however; and if they did, nothing was ever heard publicly about such protests or denunciations of the government. This silence of Church authorities sometimes gave rise to rumors among the people. From time to time, you would hear individuals angrily condemn those at the head of the Church, calling them prostitutes or communist agents. Yet for the most part everyone realized that the hierarchy and other Church authorities could not escape the pressures of the ruling regime, and the people's esteem for the Orthodox Church and its clergy remained high.

Everyone realized, too, the retaliations that would follow any attempt by the churches to oppose the government or refuse to go along with the Ministry of Cults. It was quite easy for the government. A petition would be drawn up, for instance, with a certain number of signatures, requesting that the church be closed for reasons of public order, or safety, or something of the sort. Or perhaps the city would suddenly plan some new construction project, and the church would be one of the buildings listed for demolition. Naturally, the government would always approve the petition or the new construction plan. Despite such pressures, however, despite government interference and control, despite the propaganda and the constant petty harassment that takes place in office or factory or school, the Orthodox Church continues to exert a strong influence throughout the country.

Churches that still stand or have not been closed are generally crowded, and not just with dwindling numbers of old people as the Komsomols and the League of Militant Atheists boasted, but with young people too. Some of them come to the churches precisely because they are not supposed to and, like young people everywhere, they want to show their independence. Others come at first just out of curiosity, others out of a vague desire to rediscover an ethnic or cultural link with old traditions. Many of them are searching for something, something even they do not fully understand and cannot clearly express. They know from parents or grandparents how things were in "the old days"; they wonder if they are missing something or can find something of the peace and security the "old folks" seem to have had in God. So they come. And so the faith, in God's providence, remains strong and continues to grow; baptisms continue, and even the children of some Communist Party officials are baptized in secret.

There are very few Catholic churches in Russia, except for those in the territories occupied by the Soviet Union in World War II. Most of the Catholics in Russia today, in fact, are remnants of those "volunteers" who came to the Soviet Union during the war to work as I did in the lumber camps and factories, or prisoners who have not been allowed to return to their homelands. The "parishes" I served in Norilsk are a good example; there were similar clusters of Poles or Germans or Lithuanians scattered in many of the smaller towns and villages, very few in the big cities. They were delighted to be able to have a priest among them, and the sacrifices they would make, the distances they would travel to attend Mass and the sacraments, were a continuing source of amazement and consolation to me. Otherwise, they had to attend the services held in the Orthodox churches.

Orthodox priests for the most part, though, would not permit other Christians to receive the sacrament of baptism, Holy Eucharist, or penance. In this regard, they were quite strict and most unyielding. Some of the Catholic priests of the Byzantine rite were much more open to the Orthodox faithful. We heard their confessions and baptized their children, blessed their homes, visited their sick, buried their dead. Such priests, however, were few in number. The Orthodox and Catholic faithful displayed among themselves more of that spirit which came to be known after Vatican II as ecumenism; but the churches officially still clung to the strict interpretation of laws established long ago and intended to protect the faithful from falling into error, laws that prohibited inter-communion with other Christian denominations. Such laws seemed to have little relevance to the situations in which we found ourselves in Siberia, and the faithful were the first to sense this. They wanted to worship God, to practice their religion, and to them it was the same Triune God who was worshiped and adored in the churches, the same Christ who was offered in the sacrifice of the Mass no matter which rite was celebrated. They sympathized with one another, supported one another, helped one another, told one another where a Mass would be celebrated or a priest could be found. It was they who first followed the promptings of the Spirit and broke down the barriers; it was the priests who reluctantly followed.

There were other religious sects in Siberia, as throughout the Soviet Union, some of them flourishing. They didn't build churches where they would gather for services; the homes in which they gathered on Sundays or at other times served them well enough. They kept no records of their activities. But whenever they assembled in common prayer, with readings from the Scriptures, they were somehow drawn closer together and inspired to seek out others to join them. The informality of their services, the conviction of their religious beliefs, the spontaneity of their prayers, made them aware of the presence of God in each other and in the community of believers gathered together. They were strong in their faith, not afraid to practice it or speak of it openly to others, seemingly much less afraid of persecution than other Christians or terrified by official repression. They were the bane of the secret police and the Ministry of Cults, for they refused to be intimidated — and they had no churches to confiscate. Unfortunately, they often carried this same intransigence over into their relations with other Christians; they were outspoken in their criticism of the established churches, especially the Orthodox Church and the Catholic Church. They were convinced that they alone practiced the purity of the Gospel message and looked on other Christians as sinners who needed conversion, on priests as agents of the devil or the Scarlet Woman of Babylon who led the people astray, and they said so bluntly and openly. Some of my most unpleasant experiences in the camps had been with people of this sort, and they would have little to do with me as a priest.

Nevertheless, I admired these people and the staunchness of their faith in the face of the constant propaganda and persecution that surrounded us all. I marveled often, too, at the ways of divine providence and the mysterious workings of grace in preserving the faith in Russia, despite the full might and power of an atheistic system determined to stamp out religion, despite even the all too human failings of the churches themselves. It dawned on me at such times how futile were the attempts of man or of government to destroy the kingdom of God. You can close churches, you can imprison priests and ministers, you can even set men and churches to fighting among themselves, but you cannot uproot thereby the good seed existing among the tares and cockle, that good seed which is the kingdom of God. It will remain, like the mustard seed, like the leaven in the mass. The faith of these courageous Christians in Siberia, as throughout all of Russia, was ample testimony to that.

Christ is indeed a king, as he said to Pilate, but his kingdom is not of this world. It is not a kingdom in opposition to the Soviet Government or any other government; it is not a kingdom based on territory or buildings or structures. It is a kingdom of justice and love and peace—as the Church sings in the preface of the Mass of Christ the King—a kingdom of truth and life, a kingdom of holiness and grace that exists in the hearts of men and is founded on their faith and belief in the words of Christ. "I did not come into this world to bring peace but the sword," St. Matthew records Christ as proclaiming, yet the revolution he preached was not against the powers of this world, but a revolution to be accomplished in the hearts of men. "Repent," he said, "do penance, change your hearts, for the kingdom of God is at hand."

God in his providence does not leave men at peace until they are converted in a crisis that, sooner or later, must come to every heart. God's grace demands the total transformation of man, for man belongs to God. Only in faith, only by a change of heart, can a man enter the kingdom of God. Sooner or later man must learn that this changing and unstable world cannot be the source of his security, of true peace of heart. "Seek first the kingdom of God," says the Lord, "and all these things will be added to you." *That* is the source of our ultimate peace and security—God's providence—but we must learn to accept him on faith, to seek his will in all things and follow it, to place our confidence and trust completely in him. Once we have done that, we must live in that spirit daily in all we do, in all we say, in all we think. And living in that manner, whatever we do here on earth will help to spread the kingdom of God.

Our primary responsibility, then, the main object of all our efforts, must be the transformation of ourselves, of our hearts and our lives. Insofar as we succeed at this, we promote the spreading of God's kingdom, for by doing this, we are at the same time disposing ourselves to help others and contribute even further to the spreading of the kingdom. What this means in the concrete is that each of us must faithfully fulfill the duties of our daily life. The circumstances and people that God each day presents to us through his providence offer us the opportunity to perform action after action in proof of our dedication to the kingdom. Whether we are married and taking care of home and family, or studying in school, or working in an office or a factory or on a farm, whether we are dedicated to the priestly or religious life, matters little—in whatever we do, we must always seek first the kingdom of God. That is, all of our actions of every day must be accepted as from God and referred back to him, must be done in a way that fulfills his will, for in this way alone is the kingdom of God promoted and spread upon earth.

We experience daily just how difficult it is, therefore, to promote the kingdom of God in our personal lives by fulfilling his will in every respect. No one who has tried seriously to live each day in this way will say it is an easy task. It can only be done with the help of God's grace. That grace is always given to us, but we must learn to recognize it in the people and circumstances presented to us by God's providence, in the thoughts and inspirations that tug at our minds and our hearts. We know that we do not always respond to God's grace, for his grace always demands of us sacrifice, renunciation of self-will, effort, and an untiring spirit of dedication — and the practice of these things does not come easily to the young, or the tired adult, or the old. Yet that is what the kingdom of God is all about.

Knowing how little of grace is accepted and realized in our own personal lives, we can imagine how much of his grace is spurned or rejected by those around us. In this way we come to understand, too, why there yet exists so much evil, sin, violence, wars, hatred, immorality, persecution of religion, and denial even of God himself in the world today. These things must follow, so long as men refuse to accept God's grace and do his will. The kingdom of God, reintroduced among men by the Incarnation of Christ — who came to set us a most perfect example of a man totally dedicated in all things and at all times to the will of the Father — cannot and will not be established until all men live each day of their lives according to his example.

"The kingdom of God is within you", he told us. How obvious yet how profound these words seemed to me here in Norilsk. The visible Church, which is a reflection of God's kingdom here on earth, was almost non-existent here in the vastness of Siberia. Christians here, even as I, had to attempt to serve God surrounded on all sides by an atmosphere of unbelief and godlessness, an atmosphere of atheistic propaganda that was almost suffocating. Yet my greatest consolation was the evident faith of the courageous Christians I served, a living witness in this desolate land to the power of God's grace and the existence of his kingdom. Their faith, their courage, inspired me daily to offer up all my actions and works and sufferings of each day to the work of spreading the kingdom of God upon earth. What was I, in comparison to the millions of atheists in the Soviet Union? What was I, in comparison to the might and power of the Soviet Government? What were any of us, really, in the face of the system around us, with all its organs of propaganda and powers of persecution? Yet, in God's providence, here we were. This was the place he had chosen for us, the situation and circumstances in which he had placed us. One thing we could do and do daily: we could seek first the kingdom of God and his justice—First of all in our own lives, and then in the lives of those around us. From the time of the apostles—twelve simple men, alone and afraid, who had received the commission to go forth into the whole world to preach the good news of the kingdom—there has been no other way for the spreading of the kingdom than by the acts and the lives of individual Christians striving each day to fulfill the will of God.

Chapter Eighteen

HUMILITY

An Easter ceremony will always be the highlight of my memories of Norilsk; unfortunately, it was also the cause of my leaving. The preceding Lent had seen some of the busiest weeks I've ever spent as a priest. Fathers Viktor and Neron had left Norilsk and I was alone, yet our congregation was bigger than ever. All during Lent I spent my free time hearing confessions and baptizing; on Palm Sunday I said three Masses and preached at each of them, telling the people that the full Holy Week services would be held. After the Masses on Palm Sunday, the people crowded around to make arrangements for the traditional blessing of the Easter food. Because I was alone and there was so much to do, I formed a committee of men to organize this blessing of the Easter baskets. In a special notebook we sketched out a map of the city of Norilsk, picked out certain assembly points and set specific times, so that anyone who couldn't make it to my little *bolok* could meet me there for the blessing of the food. When all the arrangements were more or less completed, I figured I would have to begin at 5 P.M. on Friday, work around the clock, and hope to finish in time for the Easter Mass.

All day Friday, I heard a tremendous number of Easter confessions, as I had every night that week after work. On Friday evening, after the Good Friday services, I set out to begin my tour of the city. Every place I went, there were people waiting—even in the middle of the night or the long cold hours of early morning. I got back to my *bolok* Saturday morning in time for services at 6 A.M. It was jammed with people, many of whom had been there overnight in order to get a place before the altar for this long

Easter Vigil service. Many of them, too, stayed in the chapel after the Saturday services until it was time for the Easter midnight Mass, with nothing to eat all day, so they could be close to the altar. After the services, I started making the rounds again, doubling back to my *bolok* every few hours to bless the baskets of food which filled my little room from wall to wall, a new batch every time. By 11:30 P.M. Saturday, I was back home but I could hardly get near the *bolok*. Even the corridors and the vestibule were jammed; crowds of people were swarming around outside in the midnight cold. There was barely room to move anywhere, but by twelve o'clock I was vested—I couldn't lift my arms because of the crowd, so someone had to pull the vestments over my head—and ready for Mass. The altar was covered with flowers and candles; we even had a choir. As I began the solemn intonation of the Easter Mass, the chapel seemed to explode with sound. An Easter Mass is a joyous one to begin with, but the enthusiasm of the people that night I shall never forget. Tired as I was after more than forty-eight hours without sleep, hurrying from place to place, I felt suddenly elated and swept along. I forgot about everything but the Mass and the joy of Easter.

The crowds were so great it was impossible to distribute Communion, because no one could move. Communion had to be distributed after Mass. The services ended at 3 A.M., but at nine o'clock the next morning I was still distributing Communion to a constant stream of people. I could hear the crowds outside, going home through the Easter dawn, shouting the traditional Easter greeting: *"Khristos voskres!"* (Christ is risen!), and the joyous answer, *"Voistinu voskres!"* (Indeed, he is risen!). After it was finally all over, I came back to my room alone and sat down at the little table in my *bolok,* completely exhausted. Yet I was deeply satisfied; I knew a joy that day I have rarely known. I felt that at last, in God's own good providence, I was beginning to live my dream of serving his flock in Russia. "And all this," was the thought that kept flashing through my mind, "all this took place in Russia, in Norilsk!"

Within the week, though, I was summoned from work to the office of the KGB. The agent in charge wasted no time. He greeted me abruptly with the statement: "Wladimir Martinovich, your missionary work here in Norilsk is not needed. Do you understand?" He told me sternly to get a ticket on the next available flight to Krasnoyarsk and to report to the KGB there. "If you attempt to come back here, you will be arrested and put into prison. I'm in charge here and those are orders." I just looked at him and said nothing. After a long pause, he said coldly: "You may leave." As I turned to leave, however, he added: "When you get your ticket, I will personally escort you to the airport."

The flight from Norilsk to Krasnoyarsk is a long one, possibly as much as four hours. I had never flown before, and I was tense and scared as the plane took off. I leaned back hard in the seat and shut my eyes, trying not to move a muscle; I could feel the drumming of the motors in my head until my ears popped, but I was even more conscious of an uneasiness at the base of my stomach. Once I got used to it, I sat there thinking of the people I was leaving behind, saddened by the thought that I could do nothing for them any longer but commend them to God. I tried hard to resist the thoughts of anger that had been burning within me since my visit to KGB headquarters, and I still felt humiliated by the way they could order me around even though I was supposed to be a free man. I consoled myself, as always, with the thought that God knew what he was doing—I kept repeating, "Thy will be done", but it was hard to understand.

After a while, as I prayed, the thought came to me that doing the will of the Father is not always an easy task—the words of our Lord I had been repeating to myself were uttered in the agony in the garden. They were Christ's own prayer just before the hours of his greatest trials and humiliations. We often use them as an example of obedience, but they are in fact the most perfect illustration of the virtue of humility. For humility, after all, is based on a very simple recognition of a fundamental truth: the true relationship between God and man. "Humility is truth" is a spiritual adage that sums it up well, for humility is nothing more or less than knowing our place before God. Christ's whole life, from birth to death, was a perfect act of humility that flowed from his total submission to the will of the Father. It reached its crest on the cross, where he died humiliated and deprived of everything. "Learn of me," he said to his disciples, "for I am meek and humble of heart." Even after a great deal of experience in the spiritual life, though, most of us are seldom humble when humiliated. We constantly need to remind ourselves of the humble Christ, the Christ who did always the will of the Father, if we are ever to learn.

It is only natural to resent humiliation. We recoil from humiliating experiences because they are an affront to the dignity of our persons—which is another way of saying that our pride is hurt. That is the key to the problem, and it is then that we do well to recall who we really are and who God is. If we see nothing beyond the experience except the hurt and the unpleasantness, it can only be because we have lost sight, for the moment at least, of God's will and of his providence. For humiliations arise out of the circumstances, situations, and people that God presents to us each day—and all these are but a manifestation of his providence. So we must learn to discern in such things, even in the humiliations, occasions for a deeper conformity to the will of God. Christ had to suffer opposition and contradiction and, yes, humiliation, in doing his Father's will; yet he was constantly intent on forgetting self entirely and glorifying the Father by his actions. If we are truly to imitate Christ in our lives, we must learn to do the same.

We must constantly return to the catechism truth we learned as children: that God made us to love, reverence, and serve him in this life and so to be happy with him in the next. We are not saved by doing our own will, but the will of the Father; we do that not by interpreting it or reducing it to mean what we would like it to mean, but by accepting it in its fullness, as made manifest to us by the situations and circumstances and persons his providence sends us. It is so simple and yet so difficult. Each day, and every minute of every day, is given to us by God with that in mind. We for our part can accept and offer back to God every prayer, work, and suffering of the day, no matter how insignificant or unspectacular they may seem to us. Yet it is precisely because our daily circumstances often seem so insignificant and unspectacular that we fail so often in this regard. It is the seeming smallness of our daily lives and the constancy of things that cause our attention and our good intentions to wander away from the realization that these things, too, are signs of God's will. Between God and the individual soul, however, there are no insignificant moments; this is the mystery of divine providence.

We see examples of this in lives around us every day. Young people planning to get married, choosing a profession, or answering a vocation to the priesthood or religious life, feel an enthusiasm and an interior joy they never knew before. Then, as the years go by, difficulties increase and there is a constant need for more sacrifice and a renewal of spirit in the initial promise or vow taken. And then it is that the test of one's humility—the realiza tion of one's place before God—really begins. Then it is that the difficulties of a man's calling begin to become a burden. "My yoke is sweet and my burden light", said Christ, but the burdens of life, the sacrifices and self-denials, the humiliations, can be so only if we see in them the express will of God. Can there be anything more consoling than to look at a burden, or a humiliation, not just as it is in itself but as the will of God entrusted to you at that moment? Viewed in that way, no matter how heavy or trying the burden or the difficulty, I am able to carry it in a spirit that indeed can make it light, for the realization that it comes from God and is his will for me carries with it a feeling of enthusiasm, of accomplishment, of importance, that brings joy and consolation to the heart.

But unfortunately those who have lost a true sense of humility— that constant realization of the relationship between each individual and God—have also lost thereby the ability to look upon their burdens in this way. They see instead only the burden, the difficulties, the humiliation; and they become depressed. They begin to pity themselves, to question things in their married lives or in their vocations that they valued highly before. Sacrifice, work, and dedication seem meaningless; charity, patience, and love become merely empty words. They begin to question now even the wisdom or the validity of their initial decision, to look for freedom or some way out. Perhaps they justify it with the data of science, or psychology, or arguments about changing times in a changing world. But ultimately, what they are trying to explain is the radical change in themselves that has brought them to the point of interior crisis in a vocation they once embraced with so much joy and enthusiasm.

How can all of this happen so suddenly, seemingly in so short a period of time? The answer lies in a loss of the virtue of humility, a loss of the vision of life as significant in God's sight, a loss of the vision that sees all things as coming from the hand of God. Once this vision is lost, then the self very subtly begins to assume greater importance and God's will begins to grow less and less important. It's not our failings or faults or sins of themselves that bring this about; it is a lack of humility. No matter how badly the humble man fails, he will reckon his accounts with God and start over again, for his humility tells him of his total dependence on God.

In this lies the difference between the truly humble person and one who lacks humility. The former sees the blame in himself for the disorders of his life, for his failures and his faults, and he strives to recapture again a sense of dedication to God's will. The latter, far from blaming himself for any faults or failings, tries to justify his actions in some way or other and persists in doing exactly those things that are slowly alienating him from God and his vocation. Even the feelings of remorse that afflict him are not seen as a grace from God to lead him back, but are interpreted instead as signs that his original decision to follow this or that vocation must somehow have been a mistake.

So I sat on the plane heading for Krasnoyarsk, asking myself why I should suddenly feel so resentful at having to leave my "parish" in Norilsk. Was it because I felt humiliated at the way I had been ordered to leave by the KGB? After all these years of trying to see God's will in the twists and turns my life had taken in spite of my own dreams and intentions (sometimes in direct contrast to what I had intended or devised), after all the years of coming gradually to see God's hand and his providence in the strange and often bitter events I had experienced, why should I now hesitate to imagine or understand that this move, too, was from God? "My ways are not your ways," says the Lord, "and my thoughts are not your thoughts; for as far as the heavens are above

the earth, so are my ways above your ways." How many times had
I finally come to understand this in reflecting on my own
experiences, how many times had I determined to try to see
always his will in all things, and would I now hesitate to accept
this abrupt end to my apostolate in Norilsk because it made no
sense to my human wisdom?

Was it really concern for the courageous Christians I was
leaving behind that saddened me, or was it personal disappointment in having to end my first really rewarding experience as a
priest, just when things seemed to be going so well? Could I
imagine, was I afraid, that God had no other way to take care of
his people? "So I will have him wait until I come", our Lord said
to Peter, "Follow thou me." Christ had called Peter aside, but Peter
was concerned about John. And now Christ, through the KGB,
was calling me from Norilsk. Why should I doubt that he would
provide somehow for those I was leaving behind—even as he had
provided for them before I came. My first concern, instead, should
be to follow wherever he led, to see his will always in the events of
my life and follow it faithfully, without question or hesitation.

Yes, I was disappointed. No, I didn't have the answers to all the
questions that plagued me, nor could I sort out completely the
thoughts that filled my mind as the plane flew closer to Krasnoyarsk,
but one thing I knew: I had long ago determined to strive to see
always his will in all things. I had promised to abandon myself
completely to his providence. This was a new day, perhaps a new
chapter in my role of spreading the kingdom, and my job was to
accept without question the situations and circumstances of this
day without looking back. This was no time, after all I had
learned and come to understand of the mysterious ways of his
providence, to begin rejecting the workings of his grace and his
will. My task this day, as always, was to yield without hesitation
and without questioning the wisdom of his will, to accept it in all
reverence without trying to make it conform to my will or
understand it fully with my limited human wisdom, to abandon
myself once again in complete trust and confidence to the mysterious workings of his grace and his wisdom.

My life, like Christ's—if my priesthood meant anything—was

to do always the will of the Father. It was humility I needed: the grace to realize my position before God—not just in times when things were going well, as they had been in Norilsk, but more so in times of doubt and disappointment, like today, when things were not going the way I would have planned them or wished them. That's what humility means—learning to accept disappointments and even defeat as God-sent, learning to persevere and carry on with peace of heart and confidence in God, secure in the knowledge that something worthwhile is being accomplished precisely because God's will is at work in our life and we are doing our best to accept and follow it.

For it is not man or what he does that counts most in the plans of divine providence, but rather that a man accepts in confidence and fulfills to the best of his ability each day what God has chosen for him. "For the foolish things of this world God chooses to confound the wise," says St. Paul, "and the weak things of this world God chooses to confound the strong." That God could use someone like myself, stubborn and sometimes stupid and full of failings, was the one thing I had learned through trial and error, through suffering and defeat, and now was no time to start backsliding. True humility consists in learning to recognize this relationship always; we must remind ourselves over and over again of the fact, for it is all too easy for proud human nature suddenly to think that this or that accomplishment is due to the efforts we made and the work we have done. And just as surely as we begin to fail in humility, we begin to lose sight of God and his grace, to exclude him to some extent from our lives.

Be thankful then, I thought to myself, that God in his loving care sends humiliations your way. Be thankful for the KGB, lest you begin to think that Easter in Norilsk was somehow your doing. It was God who planted the seed in the hearts of those people, Fathers Viktor and Neron who watered it, and it was only because God in his providence put you there at that time that you enjoyed the harvest and the consolation of those days. Be consoled, you idiot, I said to myself, but don't be fooled! It was the same God who arranged for that joy in order to strengthen and console you and who has now arranged your abrupt and humiliating departure from the scene to remind you once more that all things on this earth are governed by his providence and not man's efforts. That was yesterday, and today is today. You haven't done anything yet in the Soviet Union except by his grace and his will; every time you tried to do something on your own, to plan ahead, to work out answers beforehand, you made a miserable mess of your efforts and had to learn all over again to look for God's will in the situations and circumstances. Isn't it about time you learned? Isn't it time you learned to be meek and humble of heart, to give up your own will and strive to conform to God's, to seek first the kingdom of God and his justice—and not worry about where this plane is taking you, or what you will meet there, or what you are leaving behind?

Chapter Nineteen

FAITH

Within a week of my arrival in Krasnoyarsk, I "inherited" a parish in a way that could only confirm once again my confidence in and wonder at the workings of divine providence. I had gone to the police station to register, as instructed by the KGB chief in Norilsk, and I met there an old Lithuanian gentleman. He could tell by my accent, I guess, that I wasn't a Russian, and he asked me my nationality. I told him I was Polish. He asked me if I was Catholic. Rather guardedly, because I didn't think the police station was the place to be discussing such things, especially for me, I told him I was. He asked me if I knew any priests. Before I could answer, he told me he was a member of a parish on the outskirts of the city. There were many people in the parish, he said, but their priest had died in the past week. Now they were looking around desperately for another priest.

For a moment, I thought this might be some kind of trap arranged by the KGB; nevertheless, I continued talking with the old gentleman at length and agreed to go with him to meet some other members of the parish. I didn't tell him yet that I was a priest, but I couldn't help marveling to myself at the manner in which God arranges things. This parish on the outskirts of the city even had its own church, a big, one-story, barracklike building. The whole inside was the chapel, a long, high-ceilinged room that could accommodate more than 200 people. It had a beautifully carved altar, stations of the cross along the wall, and a confessional to one side—for all the world like a parish church anywhere. There was a sacristy behind the altar, and beyond the sacristy a room for the priest to live in. I was so delighted I wanted to move in right away!

The parishioners kept telling me how badly they needed a priest—not just for religious reasons but for political ones as well. For town officials were already talking of taking over their church building and putting it to other uses, on the grounds that the people had no priest and none was available. So when I finally told the parishioners that I was a priest, they were overjoyed. I also told them, though, about my experiences with the KGB in Norilsk, and I warned them I would surely be under close surveillance here in Krasnoyarsk. My story didn't bother them at all; they begged me to stay with them as their priest and, when I accepted, they asked me there and then to lead them in giving thanks to God for answering their prayers and sending a priest. I did so with a feeling of emotion, almost in tears, and the first little sermon I preached to them that day was on the providence of God.

The people wouldn't even hear of my getting a job; they told me how much there was to do in the parish and they promised to take care of my needs. Besides, they wanted a full-time priest. They intended to draw up a petition to the City Council, telling them that they had a priest and asking that the church not be confiscated. I was afraid of the move, frankly. I knew the city officials would want to know who the priest was and where he had come from; I was certain that my stay in Krasnoyarsk would be a short one under the circumstances. But the people were not to be dissuaded—and after what I had just seen of the workings of God's providence, I was in no position to argue for long.

They drew up the petition and asked for an appointment with the head of the City Council. He wouldn't give them a direct answer, though, or sign the necessary document; he insisted it was a matter for Moscow to handle. Undeterred, the parishioners decided to send a committee to Moscow with their petition. I was amazed at their boldness and even a little embarrassed at their faith; in fact, I was ashamed to realize that in some ways their faith was greater than mine. They never for a moment doubted that God would arrange to have their petition answered favorably— just as he had answered their prayers for another priest. And they were not afraid to stand up before the City Council, or even the Kremlin, and testify to their faith. They knew, as did people everywhere in the Soviet Union, that their actions might cost them their jobs or bring even worse reprisals, and yet they never hesitated.

How could you explain such faith in a country where atheism and fear were the order of the day? There was no explanation except the traditional one: such faith was a gift from God, as faith always is. God was a reality for these people, a reality that they clung to and placed ahead of all other personal considerations. Their faith was to them, quite literally, a matter of life and death. They were willing to sacrifice everything else for it. It was not a matter of doctrines or rules or practices for these people; it was a matter of belief and deep conviction. To them, God was as real as their own father, or brother, or best friend. They turned to him in difficulties, trusted in him, feared his judgment of their failings, and stood ready to lose everything in the world rather than offend him.

No, they weren't perfect, either as people or as Christians; they weren't saints, but their faith was a matter of principle and of practice in their lives each day. They didn't talk about it, but you could observe it in the way they approached the problems of daily living, in the way they talked about things, in the way they thought and reacted on various occasions. It was a simple faith, direct and childlike, the sort of faith our Lord praised so explicitly in the Gospels whenever he encountered it. "I have not found so great a faith in Israel", he said of the centurion, for example. That was how I felt here in the parish church of Krasnoyarsk.

Perhaps it was an old-fashioned faith. It centered for these people in the Church and the sacraments, in devotions and novenas and prayers. Perhaps it wasn't too sophisticated, and some of their ideas on good and evil, on sin and penance, on suffering and redemption, on death and resurrection, on grace and the sacraments, might not have pleased a more discriminating theologian than I was. But it was also a faith that had been tested and purified in the fire of constant low-keyed persecution, had been attacked and ridiculed by atheist propagandists on all sides and at every level—

and it had survived. It was too precious a thing to these simple people to be traded away in exchange for social advancement, or a better job, or even in exchange for the best education for their children, whom they dearly loved. For them, faith was a way of life; it was at the center of their life, of their day, and of all their actions. They rarely discussed it or argued about it with others, they probably could not have explained their beliefs very well if they tried, but it was there at the heart of their being; they believed in God and his Church. They trusted in him, turned to him in difficulties, gave thanks to him in moments of happiness, and fully expected to be with him for all eternity.

That is the faith we all share, of course. We did not merit it—God gave it to us as a free gift—but it is ours to preserve or to lose. It is ours to cherish or to take for granted, and if we begin to take it for granted we will surely lose it. So we must strive instead to be ever more conscious of it, to be jealous of it and guard it, even as the Jews from Old Testament times until today cherished and still jealously guard the realization of their selection as God's chosen people, even as these simple Christians of Krasnoyarsk guarded and practiced their faith. We must make it the unspoken principle that guides our every action, the center of our being and of all that we do each day. It must become as real for us, as necessary to our lives, as the air we breathe—for without it our lives have no meaning and our soul may die. We must constantly work to strengthen it and make it operative in all we do.

The surest way to do this, I think, is by prayer. In prayer we speak to God, we ask his help, we seek his pardon or we promise amends, we thank him for favors received. But we cannot pray as if we were talking to the empty air; so in the very act of praying we unconsciously remind ourselves of the reality and the presence of God, thereby strengthening our belief in him. And that is why, again in my opinion, the Morning Offering is still one of the best practices of prayer—no matter how old-fashioned some may think it. For in it, at the beginning of each day, we accept from God and offer back to him all the prayers, works, and sufferings of the day, and so serve to remind ourselves once again of his providence and his kingdom. If we could only remember to spend the day in his presence, in doing his will, what a difference it would make in our own lives and the lives of those around us! We cannot pray always, in the sense of those contemplatives who have dedicated their whole lives to prayer and penance. Nor can we go around abstracted all day, thinking only of God and ignoring our duties to those around us, to family and friends and to those for whom we are responsible. But we *can* pray always by making each action and work and suffering of the day a prayer insofar as it has been offered and promised to God.

Moreover, we are not alone in our faith. We are members of the Church, the Mystical Body, the kingdom of God here on earth. We are members of this Church through baptism—the sacrament of the life of faith—and it is in and through the Church that Christ has given us the means to strengthen our faith: his sacraments. They were the means established by Christ precisely to strengthen the faith of his followers. If we are serious about preserving *our* faith, we must surely make use of them—especially the sacrament of penance, our means of peace and of reconciliation with God, and the Mass and the sacrament of the Eucharist.

Yet the Church is more than a sacramental system, it is a community of believers, a Mystical Body, the kingdom of God here on earth. As members of that body, we cannot remain aloof or indifferent to others or to the good of the whole. Each of us must do his part to strengthen this body and extend this kingdom. Our personal lives, then, cannot be developed apart from the Church. Whether we experience a crisis in our own lives or sometimes feel alienated by other Christians, we do wrong both to ourselves and the Mystical Body of Christ if we leave the Church. Whatever the problem, we have an obligation flowing from the faith we share to seek a solution within the Church and not outside it. We simply cannot separate our personal lives from that of Christ, or from the body of which he is the head, because of some personal feeling of dissatisfaction or hurt. We cannot naïvely pretend that God can be found anywhere—that he can be served and loved and invoked as Savior—and ignore the Church he founded. The Church is full of human failings because it is composed of human beings; it has its share of scandals and bad leaders, of mediocre minds, of selfishness and skin-deep spirituality, of fallible and imperfect men who do not always practice what they preach. Nevertheless, it remains the institution Christ founded to preserve and guard the faith, the Mystical Body wherein even the weak can be made strong.

A man of faith is always conscious of God, not only in his own life but in the lives of others. This is the basis of true charity, of that great commandment by which we are instructed to "love God with our whole mind and our whole heart and our whole soul, and our neighbor as ourselves". Faith, then, is the basis for love; it is in the insight of faith that we understand the fatherhood of God and the brotherhood of all men. Love, St. John writes repeatedly, is the one thing that fulfills all the commandments and the law. But prior to love, and bolstering it at the core, is faith; we must have faith before we can love, or we will surely end up loving the wrong thing—loving ourselves more than God, or loving creatures for themselves—and this is the meaning of sin. To increase our love, to love properly, we must strive always to increase our faith, and we do this by means of prayer and the sacraments.

Jesus himself, in the midst of his busy public life, would withdraw from his disciples and retire to the mountains to pray. We must follow his example if we wish to preserve and strengthen our faith, to keep constantly before our minds the fact that our whole life is from God and a going to God, to be ever mindful of his will in all that we do. By prayer, we refer to God all that happens in our life each day, whether good or ill. For there is no difference between a man of faith and a man without faith (or of little faith) with respect to the routine experiences all of us undergo every moment of our lives, day in and day out, for weeks and months and years at a time. Our lives externally are little different from the lives of those around us; what makes the difference, what *must* make the difference, is the faith that inspires all our decisions and choices and actions. Without faith, our lives are just so many empty and boring routines, hollow at the core, as day succeeds day with little sense of meaning or feeling of accomplishment. With faith, however, even the most boring and routine action of every day has merit and significance for us—and for the kingdom of God.

There are moments of crisis in every life, moments of anxiety and fear, moments of frustration and opposition, moments sometimes even of terror. The kingdom of Christ—that kingdom of justice and peace, of love and of truth—has not yet been achieved here on earth; it has begun, but much remains to be done before it can reach its fullness and all creation will have again been made new according to the mind of the Father. Evil still exists alongside justice like the cockle among the wheat, hatred alongside love, the bad with the good, the sinner along with the saint. None of us, then, can escape the tensions of this imperfect world—neither sinner nor saint, bad or good, the weak or the strong, the sick or the healthy, the simple or the learned, the indifferent or the dedicated. Only by a lively faith can a man learn to live in peace among the tensions of this world, secure in his ability (with God's help) to weather the crises of life, whenever they come and whatever they may be, for he knows that God is with him. In the midst of suffering or failure or even sin, when he feels lost or overwhelmed by danger or temptation, his faith still reminds him of God. By faith he has learned to lift himself above the circumstances of this life and to keep his eyes fixed upon God, from whom he expects the grace and the help he needs, no matter how unworthy he may feel.

Faith, then, is the fulcrum of our moral and spiritual balance. The problems of evil or of sin, of injustice, of sufferings, even of death, cannot upset the man of faith or shake his trust and confidence in God. His powerlessness to solve such problems will not be a cause of despair or despondency for him, no matter how strong his concern and anxiety may be for himself and for those around him. At the core of his being there exists an unshakable confidence that God will provide, in the mysterious ways of his own divine providence.

And yet faith also teaches him that he cannot be indifferent, that he cannot just shrug his shoulders and sigh, "God will provide." He knows that he must, in the words of one spiritual maxim, "work as if everything depended upon him and pray as if everything depended upon God." He recognizes that it was by the Incarnation that the kingdom of God was established. For it was in the mystery of his Incarnation that God became man in order to set us the most perfect example—and to teach us by this example how his kingdom must be extended on earth. The kingdom of God will grow upon earth, will be brought to fulfillment, in the same way it was established: by the daily and seemingly hidden lives of those who do always the will of the Father.

It was this faith that impressed me so much in the Christians of Krasnoyarsk and in the other believers I met in the Soviet Union, whether Orthodox, Baptists, Evangelicals, or the members of various sects I came in contact with. Hampered by difficulties and every form of subtle persecution, restricted by law, they nevertheless retained their belief in God and all that it meant in practice. Their prayers and their sufferings can only foreshadow, I know, a future harvest of faith in this land once known as Holy Russia. The kingdom of God survives and is spread by the active and unshakable faith of such people as these; it remains, too, in the hearts of the masses who know instinctively there must be more to life than the future promised by communism. No one knows better than those who are constantly attacking that faith how firmly its seeds remain planted in Russia; only God in his providence knows how soon it will flower.

Chapter Twenty

HUMANITY

My stay at the parish in Krasnoyarsk didn't last very long. The secret police showed up one morning at 1 A.M. and gave me forty-eight hours to get out of town. They didn't waste time in argument or explanation. They simply stamped my permit to live in Krasnoyarsk "canceled" and told me I would be arrested if I was still there two days later. They ignored my questions and went about the proceedings quite matter-of-factly, for the most part in silence. When they had finished, the agent in charge said with cold precision: "Wladimir Martinovich, you have been warned repeatedly and this is your last chance. You can either go to Abakan or Yeniseisk, that's all." I had never heard of either town, but he told me Yeniseisk was in northern Siberia and Abakan to the South. I had had enough of northern Siberia, so I chose Abakan. "Very well," he said, "now let me make one thing clear: in Abakan you will do no more of the work you've been doing here and in Norilsk—or else you will wind up where you started. Do I make myself clear?" He didn't say anything about being a priest or about religion, but we both knew what he meant.

Accordingly, when I got to Abakan I went to work at the city garage, ATK-50, and found a room as a lodger in the home of an invalid and his wife. Ironically, he was a man who before his illness had been the secretary of the City Council, a party man and still a staunch communist. Because he was an invalid and living on a small pension, however, he and his wife were happy to rent me their spare room in order to supplement the family income, even though I was a bit vague on how and why I had come to Abakan and how long I intended to stay.

I lived with him and his wife for more than two years, until he told me with embarrassment and chagrin that his old cronies at the City Council had been asking about me and "suggesting" that it didn't look good for a party man like himself to have someone like me living with him. By that time we were good friends, and he was deeply ashamed to ask me to move; yet he was also concerned about losing his membership in the party and his meager pension. By that time too, though, I had made many friends in the neighborhood and it was easy enough for us to arrange that I should move in with the family next door, who were also good friends. I was delighted with the arrangement, for I had grown fond of these people who treated me like a member of the family and I was glad to remain close to them. Moreover, my new lodgings also afforded me somewhat more privacy and a better chance to say Mass each day without fear of interruption. There was generally no one home in the new house when I finished my shift at the garage except for *Babushka,* the old grandmother, and so I usually had an opportunity before dinner for Mass or quiet prayer. *Babushka* and I quickly became great friends, and she always had a cup of hot soup or kasha waiting for me when I came home at night.

These years in Abakan were my first real chance to become intimately involved with daily life and family life in the Soviet Union. I spent long hours in conversation with these families and their friends, and I came to know a good cross section of people — from the workers I knew at the garage and elsewhere, all the way up to party men who were constantly dropping in to chat with their former City Council colleague. His home, in fact, was a meeting place of sorts, with a constant stream of visitors. That too was an advantage for me, for people could come to visit and talk with me privately about religion without calling much attention to themselves or to me in the constant goings and comings around the house. At first I was extremely cautious here in Abakan not to mention that I was a priest or to engage in any apostolate. But little by little it became known; friend told friend and soon I was busy again. Not, however, in any formal way or with large groups, but with individuals and couples. I gave advice, I counseled,

I heard confessions and baptized children, I anointed the sick and the dying. Once again, I was amazed at the faith and the constancy of these people and the sacrifices they were willing to make for their faith. And I grew to love these Russian people as never before. The ordinary Soviet citizen is not taken in by all the propaganda. Like any human being, he yearns for a richer and fuller life, he seeks a deeper meaning to life than the material things promised (but not yet delivered) by communism or the "glorious revolution" of building the perfect socialistic society. He is proud of his country's achievements, proud of what has been accomplished in a few short generations, and he doesn't much question the system he lives under. But he and his friends are troubled by the same problems as people everywhere, and they are looking for answers. They are not sure religion is the answer, indeed they are suspicious of religion and the churches, but they are looking for more satisfactory answers to their inner longing and questions than communism has yet offered.

By its very ideology, communism concerns itself with the question of humanity; to this end it directs all its efforts. No social system in the world gives such prestige to man as does communism, at least in theory and in propaganda. Literature, culture, education, work, science, law, medicine, labor, and all the riches of the country are meant to serve the good of the people. There are slogans everywhere that read, "All for man." Gorky's saying that the word *man* resounds beautifully is often quoted, and children in school and workers in factories are repeatedly told there is nothing in the world more precious than the human being called man. Special expressions in daily usage have been created to emphasize the goodness of human nature. A whole morality has been constructed on the subject, and it permeates the new social order. When reprimanded by authorities or by a comrade for some failure or wrongdoing, citizens are reminded of their obligation to be human, to be conscientious human beings, honest, men of their word. These basic characteristics of human nature are constantly instilled in the minds of children and all Soviet citizens with a fierce insistence. The communist man, the man of the new social order, must be superior to all human beings, for on him depends the conversion of the world to communism, to freedom and brotherhood and justice for all.

The party and the government use every means at their disposal to educate citizens in this new spirit of communism. All the communications media, the theaters, art and literature, the schools and labor unions and clubhouses built all over the country for that very purpose stress the same theme. Even entertainment and art are not free from this frequently annoying insistence on the virtues of the new communist man: on the dignity of work for a cause, on the need for honesty and the observance of law, on brotherhood and on the necessity to give and accept fraternal comradely correction. The highest ideas of human love and charity are stressed; selfishness and sloth and greed are the chief enemies. The goal is to provide for the common good of all, to do for humanity what mankind has never yet succeeded in doing.

There is no doubt that such constant propaganda has an effect. One obvious achievement is a spirit of comradeship unrealized anywhere else. Another is the very real pride the people take in their accomplishment, whether it be the fulfillment of a five-year plan, or the construction of a new dam or factory, or a good harvest, or simply of having filled the daily norms set for their individual jobs. A sense of having enriched the motherland in some way or other makes people feel a part of things and proud of the system. They cannot understand capitalism and say so openly. They have heard their system and their achievements extolled over and over again through a generation, and they have come to believe it; they simply take it for granted and think that somehow or other that's the way things must be. Nor is there anything surprising about this. In the West the same psychological effect is produced by advertising all sorts of new products—cars, homes, soaps and deodorants, styles, or even pornography. The American way of life is pictured in full color, and people come to believe they must have these things—even to the extent of going into debt or getting a loan in order to have the latest and feel up to date with the latest styles or developments.

Yet none of these things really satisfy people. Perhaps there is an unconscious, conditioned-reflex acceptance of the premises and goals so constantly repeated, but there is also a vaguely realized and perhaps equally unconscious feeling that there must be more to life than material possessions and accomplishments, whether individual or collective. Over and over again, I took part in discussions with ordinary workers and husbands and wives and grandmothers of families, from the most simple to the most sophisticated communists, on the meaning of life and the question of morality. It wasn't necessary for me to initiate these discussions; the constant repetition of the slogan "All for man" is the communist equivalent of TV commercials, or a news report or documentary or even some cultural program or piece of entertainment, was enough to trigger reactions and start the discussions.

The betterment of mankind, the abstract notion of humanity, or a glorified concept of man are very tenuous ideals that quickly lose their power to inspire or to satisfy in the face of daily experience and the constant grind of day-to-day living. One can be dedicated for a while to the goal of serving suffering humanity, one can be inspired by the notion of brotherhood as a goal, but human nature being what it is—and human failings all too prevalent—it is difficult to support and maintain these moments of inspiration without some deeper and more significant motivation. In Marxist ideology, in atheistic communism, man and the material world are all there is; for the rest, there is only a vague vision of some future perfect society, some more elevated and better stage of mankind that will exist in a golden age to come for which even the most doctrinaire apologists of communism have long since given up trying to set a date. Suddenly, today's communists find themselves in the position of those first- and second-century Christians who began to realize that the Parousia, the second coming of Christ, was not just around the corner. Ironically, the future golden age of communism is now treated by the ordinary citizen, and especially the young, with the same contempt that communist spokesmen used to reserve for their "pie in the sky" descriptions of religion.

Man, after all, is only man—especially if he is the fellow next door with all his petty failings, or the stupid guy at the next workbench on the job, or the cheating butcher or shop clerk, the discourteous and impatient bus driver, the rude and ill-tempered traffic policeman, the shouting party member or social climber, the bad-tempered shop foreman or union boss, the neighbor's undisciplined spoiled brats. You can sympathize with the sick and the suffering and be moved to help them, you can be stirred by the stories of victims of war or natural catastrophes, but it's hard to feel much sympathy or brotherly love for those with whom you rub elbows every day and observe with all too human failings. What claim does the man on the street have on me? Why should I treat that ape down the block or at work as a "comrade" out of some noble but totally abstract idea of brotherhood? Love for family and friends is one thing—it springs from something inside human nature and the bonds of mutual sharing and sacrifice—but love for mankind in general, what is that?

And how could you explain the larger evils of communism? These people knew of the terrors of Stalin's time; practically everyone in our group had a friend or a relative or at least knew of someone who had been to the slave labor camps of Siberia. Where was the system's much vaunted "humanity" then? Or abortions. Just take abortions. Here in our little town alone there were fifty-six abortions daily—just check the official statistics— and what about the rest of the Soviet Union? Is that any way to foster humanity?

Abortion is legal in the Soviet Union. Anyone who wants one can have it performed. The government says it had to be legalized in order to prevent private abuses. The wages of husband and wife together make it hard to support more than one or two children, so everyone wants an abortion. Yet the question haunts them. The hallways of the clinics adjoining the abortion rooms were full of posters, not praising abortion but informing patients of the possible detrimental effects on both mind and body such an operation could have. The doctors, mostly women, and the nurses and other personnel would try to dissuade patients from the operation. Women confided years later that they could not rid themselves of feelings of guilt about it. And these were not "believers", but women and girls who had received a complete atheistic education in Soviet schools.

Even for communism, it is a basic question of life and death, of wrong and right. If life at its very root can be treated so lightly, people would say, who is going to stop such a mentality from spreading? Society? Hardly. Society cannot even handle properly its present problems of crime and other social disorders. And when a society actually endorses evil, where will it end? Can man alone be trusted to solve mankind's problems? Look at history, and the depths to which civilized countries have sunk, time after time.

Little by little, in such conversations, I would bring in the notion of God and religion, of fallen human nature and redemption, of Christ and his kingdom. Of course, it depended on whom I was with and how ready they were to listen as to how far I would go or what I would say. My closest friends knew I was a priest and would sometimes listen eagerly; with others, I would simply state unashamedly that I was a "believer" and wait for their reaction to see where the conversation might lead.

Some were curious and would question me further, some would just shrug, and some would bitterly attack religion and the Church. Their attacks would always center on the abuses that are the highlight of all atheistic propaganda against religion: the greed of the Church and how the priests and monks sell candles and icons for money, the sexual perversions of priests and nuns, the political influence and power politics of the Church under the Tsars, the weird ascetical practices and penances of "holy men", even the tortures of the Inquisition. Every charge that the Church or churchmen have ever left themselves open to by their human failings is recounted in great detail in the courses on atheism in the schools and displayed in the public museums of atheism. That is the only side of the Church the ordinary citizen of this generation has ever heard about, so his antipathy to the Church and to religion, based on these half-truths and distortions, is understandable. I didn't try to defend these things—God alone knows whether they can be defended—but tried instead to steer the conversation back to the truths of faith that had some bearing on our earlier conversation about the meaning of life and the brotherhood of man.

I talked about God as I believed in him, about creation and God's plan for man and the world. I talked about the Fall and about sin, of man's rejection of God and his plan, of the disorder that had come into the world and the evils that had plagued the human race because of this disorder we call sin. I talked about God's promise of a redeemer, and the coming of Christ. I spoke of the example he set us of one perfect human life, in which every thought and action was dedicated to doing God's will, the will of the Father, and so restoring again that perfect order which had originally been God's plan for all mankind. I talked of how he had suffered every indignity a human being could suffer, from a humble birth, to poverty, to thirty years of the dullest and most routine life of work in a small and backward village, to rejection and suffering and pain and finally death, the end that faces every man. I spoke of his resurrection and victory over death—that central fact of all Christian belief which gives us absolute assurance of life beyond death, of life beyond this life, the assurance that there is a meaning to man and to his existence here on earth that transcends death.

I told of how his coming was the beginning of a new age, of a new kingdom, the beginning—but only the beginning—of a re-creation of the world according to God's original plan which all of us now must dedicate ourselves to perfect and bring to completion. I explained his teaching on the fatherhood of God, which alone made sense of the brotherhood of man, of his teachings on love and justice and truth and honesty and self-sacrifice and conformity to the will of God, which form the basis of Christian morality and the perfecting of the kingdom Christ had come to establish upon earth. Finally, I spoke of faith and the hope it gave to men, not only of a better future life, of "pie in the sky bye and bye", but of the possibility of redeeming this world and all mankind.

I wasn't out to convert anybody, but those themes were my contributions to the discussions that arose spontaneously about the meaning of life and of humanity, about brotherhood and a sense of dedication to work for a better life, about evil in the world and morality, about freedom and peace. If I didn't make believers out of anyone in the course of these rambling conversations, I at least presented them with an alternative to the party line and the doctrines they had heard and come to believe and sometimes question. I offered another answer at least to the questions that troubled them, and made them aware that for those of us who believed, at any rate, there was a meaning to man and his existence here on earth that went beyond the purely human and material. It wasn't a matter of telling them that I had all the answers and they had all the questions and problems; I was trying to show that the doubts and the longings expressed, the inner stirrings of their hearts and souls, came from a spirit in man that was natural but more than material. I echoed St. Augustine's saying that man's heart was made for God alone and it is restless until it comes to rest in him. Nor was it a question of my giving long sermons or explanations of the Church's doctrine or the Creed or salvation history—as the above synopsis might make it seem—for the evenings were filled with questions and counter-questions, with arguments and rebuttals, with explanations that led to further thoughts and questions and explanations, and generally with good humor underlying honest sincerity.

Most ordinary Russian citizens know that religion still exists in the country, and many of them are eager to learn more about it. Many of them, too, can still recall how their parents and their grandparents clung to traditional beliefs and practices, how they wanted the children at least baptized, and they recall with a mixture of fondness and nostalgia the goodness of that generation they were later taught to ridicule in school because of the "superstitious" beliefs. Was it religion, they now asked themselves, that made those old folks good people? And what was it that made them go to their death still believing? They wonder, as well, what there is about religion that prompts the neighbors and fellow workers they know about to continue practicing their faith in the face of ridicule and harassment, of petty persecution and loss of social privileges, of personal suffering and sacrifice. Is there really something to it, they ask, and can it really matter so much, make so much difference to a man's life?

The example of such courageous Christians, the curiosity and questions they inspire, do not make many converts—nor did my long conversations and explanations. But they must surely prepare the ground for the seeds of faith, which God alone can plant in the hearts of men. God, in the wonderful ways of his divine providence, uses many means to attain his end. Even communism itself, though its express aim is the destruction of religion and all belief in God, has a purpose in his plan. It is ruthless and cruel and violent, but it has also destroyed much that was corrupt and has started to build a new society dedicated, ironically, to humanity. On a purely natural level, its concern for man has done much good; its people, through suffering—and, undoubtedly, much unnecessary suffering—have responded to its harsh demands with a great deal of self-sacrifice, in a spirit of dedication and a sense of brotherhood that might well be the envy of many a more Christian country. Surely the seeds of faith that God will plant in his own good time must find in such hearts as these a fertile soil and a rich harvest at last.

My apostolate to these people, again in the strange and mysterious ways of divine providence, has ended. But I remember them with fondness and sadness; I pray for them daily. I still remember them along with my Russian Christians of Norilsk and Krasnoyarsk, with my fellow prisoners and friends in the labor camps, in my Mass each morning—and I offer up all the prayers, works, and sufferings of each day for their eternal salvation and happiness with God. That is my role in the kingdom now as then, in conformity with God's will for me, and I accept and embrace it daily as I have ever done.

EPILOGUE

I have written much in this book about the will of God and his providence. I am afraid some readers may feel that I have made too much of it, and to them I can only apologize. Others may feel that my beliefs in this matter are too simple, even naïve; they may find that my faith is not only childlike but childish. I am sorry if they feel this way, but I have written only what I know and what I have experienced. Many people, from newsmen to housewives, asked me over and over again how I managed to survive the years in Soviet prisons and the labor camps of Siberia. My answer has always been—and can only be—that I survived on the basis of the faith others may find too simple and naïve. So I have offered this explanation in answer to the many questions asked of me, in the hope that it might prove helpful to those who were interested or seeking an answer. To those who feel disappointed, who find it hard to accept so simple an explanation, who had perhaps hoped to hear from me some secret and mysterious formula that would help change their lives or strengthen their faith and cannot accept what I have written, I can only express my regrets and my sympathy.

Perhaps my words might have more meaning to some if I were a theologian and could better explain the workings of grace and the movements of the soul I have learned only by experience, but I am not and cannot. All I can do is state as plainly and as honestly as I know how the simple truths I myself learned only by trial and error, truths that I came only gradually to appreciate even in my own life after much anguish of soul and a great deal of prayerful reflection, truths that sustained me finally through the long years of doubt and darkness, of hardship and suffering. It is my hope, indeed my prayer, that what I have learned and come to understand so slowly and painfully might be of service to others. God is a very patient teacher, and I was a most stubborn pupil. I am convinced, though, that he taught me the lessons I have tried to repeat in this book not for myself alone, but that through them I could be of help to others. It was in that belief I set out to write this book, conscious of the limited ability at my command and all too aware that I have no special claim to a hearing or to credibility, yet convinced that one purpose at least (in the mysterious workings of his divine providence) for my return from the Soviet Union was to tell the story I have tried to tell here. Somewhat like Isaiah, I am embarrassed about it all, but driven nevertheless to speak what I have been given to speak.

For all my apologies, therefore, I am not ashamed of what I have written here—simple as some may find it. The terrible thing about all divine truth, indeed, is its simplicity. Whether it be the secrets of the physical universe he has created (like Einstein's $E = mc^2$), or the Ten Commandments, or the Beatitudes, or the truth we learned in the catechism—all can be simply stated. And yet how curious it is that this very simplicity makes them so unacceptable to the wise and the proud and the sophisticated of this world. "It is the simple things of this world", says St. Paul, "that God has chosen to confound the wise." Has God really planned it so, or is it just that we in our human wisdom are too proud to accept the utter simplicity of divine wisdom? Why must we always look for more sophisticated, more meaningful, more relevant answers, when he has set the truth before us in so stark and simple a fashion?

Man was created to praise, reverence, and serve God in this world and to be happy with him forever in the next. That is the fact of the matter; you believe it or you don't—and that is the end of it. Philosophers may argue about it, and they have; some have managed to convince themselves and others of its truth, while others have not. But it is the first truth of the faith, and those who have faith accept it; those who do not, do not. I cannot myself convince anyone of it, but I believe it. I do not apologize for my faith, nor am I ashamed of it.

What I have tried to show in the pages of this book, however, is how that faith has affected my life and sustained me in all I experienced. That faith is the answer to the question most often asked of me ("How did you manage to survive?") and I can only repeat it, simply and unashamedly. To me, that truth says more than that man has a duty and obligation toward his Creator, as many have tended to interpret it. To me, it says that God has a special purpose, a special love, a special providence for all those he has created. God cares for each of us individually, watches over us, provides for us. The circumstances of each day of our lives, of every moment of every day, are provided for us by him. Let the theologians argue about how this is so, let the philosophers and sophisticates of this world question and doubt whether it can be so; the revealed truth we have received on God's own word says simply that it is so. But maybe we are all just a little afraid to accept it in all its shattering simplicity, for its consequences in our lives are both terrible and wonderful.

It means, for example, that every moment of our life has a purpose, that every action of ours, no matter how dull or routine or trivial it may seem in itself, has a dignity and a worth beyond human understanding. No man's life is insignificant in God's sight, nor are his works insignificant—no matter what the world or his neighbors or family or friends may think of them. Yet what a terrible responsibility is here. For it means that no moment can be wasted, no opportunity missed, since each has a purpose in man's life, each has a purpose in God's plan. Think of your day, today or yesterday. Think of the work you did, the people you met, moment by moment. What did it mean to you—and what might it have meant for God? Is the question too simple to answer, or are we just afraid to ask it for fear of the answer we must give?

The air is full these days with talk of peace, of commitment, of fulfillment. Yet no one can know greater peace, no one can be more committed, no one can achieve a greater sense of fulfillment in his life than the man who believes in this truth of the faith and strives daily to put it into practice. If it all seems too simple, you have only to try it to find how difficult it is. But you have only to try it to find out as well the joy and the peace and the happiness it can bring. For what can ultimately trouble the soul that accepts every moment of every day as a gift from the hands of God and strives always to do his will? "If God is for us, who can stand against us?" Nothing, not even death, can separate us from God. Nothing can touch us that does not come from his hand, nothing can trouble us because all things come from his hand. Is this too simple, or are we just afraid really to believe it, to accept it fully and in every detail of our lives, to yield ourselves up to it in total commitment? This is the ultimate question of faith, and each must answer it for himself in the quiet of his heart and the depths of his soul. But to answer it in the affirmative is to know a peace, to discover a meaning to life, that surpasses all understanding.

That is the only secret I have come to know. It is not mine alone; Christ himself spoke of it, the saints have practiced it, others have written about it far better than I. I can only hope that what I have written will strike a responsive chord in some, will prove a help to others, however few. And I pray that you may be one of them.